AMIS AND AMILOUN, ROBERT OF CISYLE, AND SIR AMADACE

MIDDLE ENGLISH TEXTS SERIES

The Middle English Texts Series is designed for classroom use. Its goal is to make available to teachers and students texts that occupy an important place in the literary and cultural canon but have not been readily available in student editions. The series does not include those authors, such as Chaucer, Langland, or Malory, whose English works are normally in print in good student editions. The focus is, instead, upon Middle English literature adjacent to those authors that teachers need in compiling the syllabuses they wish to teach. The editions maintain the linguistic integrity of the original work but within the parameters of modern reading conventions. The texts are printed in the modern alphabet and follow the practices of modern capitalization, word formation, and punctuation. Manuscript abbreviations are silently expanded, and *u/v* and *j/i* spellings are regularized according to modern orthography. Yogh (ȝ) is transcribed as *g*, *gh*, *y*, or *s*, according to the sound in Modern English spelling to which it corresponds; thorn (þ) and eth (ð) are transcribed as *th*. Distinction between the second person pronoun and the definite article is made by spelling the one *thee* and the other *the*, and final *-e* that receives full syllabic value is accented (e.g., *charité*). Hard words, difficult phrases, and unusual idioms are glossed on the page, either in the right margin or at the foot of the page. Explanatory and textual notes appear at the end of the text, often along with a glossary. The editions include short introductions on the history of the work, its merits and points of topical interest, and brief working bibliographies.

Amis and Amiloun, Robert of Cisyle, and Sir Amadace

Edited by
Edward E. Foster

SECOND EDITION

Published for TEAMS
(The Consortium for the Teaching of the Middle Ages)
in Association with the University of Rochester

by

MEDIEVAL INSTITUTE PUBLICATIONS
Kalamazoo, Michigan
2007

Library of Congress Cataloging-in-Publication Data

Amis and Amiloun, Robert of Cisyle, and Sir Amadace / edited by
Edward E. Foster. -- 2nd ed.
        p. cm. -- (Middle English Texts series)
    Includes bibliographical references.
    ISBN 978-1-58044-125-4 (pbk. : alk. paper)
    1.   Romances, English. 2. English poetry--Middle English,
1100-1500. 3. Knights and knighthood--Poetry. I. Foster, Edward
E.
    PR2064.A65 2007
    821'.0330801--dc22   2007006119

ISBN 978-1-58044-125-4

Contents

 ACKNOWLEDGMENTS

ACKNOWLEDGMENTS FOR THE FIRST EDITION

I would like to thank the National Library of Scotland for the use of the Auchinleck Manuscript (Advocates MS. 19.2.1) as the basis for my text of *Amis and Amiloun* and the Scolar Press whose 1977 facsimile in fact gave me access to the manuscript; the British Library for copying MS Egerton 2862, fols. 135–37 and 145–47, which I have used as the basis for the beginning and ending of *Amis and Amiloun*; the Bodleian Library for the use of the Vernon Manuscript (MS. Eng. Poet. A1) as the basis for my text of *Robert of Cisyle* and Boydell and Brewer, Ltd., whose 1987 facsimile in fact gave me access to the manuscript; and the Princeton University Libraries for the use of Taylor Ms. 9, fols. 16–33 from the Robert H. Taylor Collection for *Sir Amadace*.

I am grateful to Mara Amster at the University of Rochester for her review of my text against its sources and for numerous and profound improvements in readings and textual notes, especially in *Sir Amadace*; to Eve Salisbury and Jennifer Church for setting the format of the volume; and to Russell Peck and Alan Lupack for their critique of the volume. Tom Seiler and Juleen Eichinger likewise reviewed the final version of my manuscript. I am also grateful to the National Endowment for the Humanities for their support during the editorial process.

ACKNOWLEDGMENTS FOR THE SECOND EDITION

Kristi J. Castleberry, Valerie B. Johnson, and Daniel Stokes of the University of Rochester reviewed recent scholarship and researched additional notes. John H. Chandler reviewed the volume and reset the format. Patricia Hollahan and the staff of MIP brought the volume to completion.

INTRODUCTION TO *AMIS AND AMILOUN*

The story of Amis and Amiloun was popular in many versions throughout Europe, but the Middle English version is especially lively, entertaining, and perplexing. The pace of the narrative, despite its frequent formulaic language, has a forward impulse that drives the characters from one moral dilemma to another with speed and clarity. The twelve-line stanza, rhyming *aabaabccdeed*, effectively presses the development of the action. The basic structure is a series of interrelated challenges which culminate in a predictable, though not fully earned, happy ending. That the happy ending is not earned is not a narrative flaw but the ultimate moral complexity that the poem proposes. Amis and Amiloun are taken out of the simple world of romance, in which the hero is exactly what his world calls for and rewards. Although they finally succeed, Amis and Amiloun's values are scrutinized all along the way.

The premise of the story is the deep and abiding friendship of Amis and Amiloun first manifested in their mutual pledge of "trewthe," total loyalty and fidelity. Such pledges were apparently common, and elaborate descriptions of them ornament many romances. The profound vow of friendship is the foundation of the poem's narrative structure and moral exploration. The pledge derives its power and authenticity from the way it is embedded in the poem: Amis and Amiloun, born on the same day, so physically alike that they are distinguishable only by their clothing, put to the service of "the duke" together at age twelve, and simultaneously knighted at fifteen, are almost identical in their behavior as young "flowers of chivalry." It thus seems natural and proper that they should promise perpetual fidelity to each other.

Although the immediate source of the poem as a whole is undeterminable, the pledge probably came through a chanson de gestes version but ultimately from more distant and diverse origins in folklore. The pledge itself is tested and its significance probed by confrontation with a variety of other familiar motifs from folklore: an evil steward, a persistent wooer, trial by combat, a test of chastity, punishment by leprosy, and infant sacrifice. Of course, these folkloric motifs had been long incorporated into the fabric of medieval narrative and are observable in romance, legend, ballad, and hagiography. Indeed, there are versions of *Amis and Amiloun* which are more strongly hagiographic than our poem is, in that the resolution is clearly attributable, say, to a "miracle of the Virgin." Such is not the case in this narrative. The Middle English *Amis and Amiloun* lodges the problem directly in the vow the two companions make and the consequences of the playing out of that pledge in unpredictable circumstances. As one might expect in folklore, the precise language is significant:

On a day the childer, war and wight,	*alert and brave*
Trewethes togider thai gun plight	*Pledged their loyalty together*
While thai might live and stond	

1

> That bothe bi day and bi night,   *by*
> In wele and wo, in wrong and right,   *good and ill*
> That thai schuld frely fond   *nobly try*
> To hold togider at everi nede,   *to stick together*
> In word, in werk, in wille, in dede . . .   (lines 145–52)

The implicit perils of such a promise should be clear — and the essence of it is repeated when they part from each other. The pledge is to be maintained even when it comes into conflict with competing moral values, which it does in a succession of events, each familiar in itself, but intensified and complicated by the context of the solemn pledge. The structural elegance of the poem and its moral sophistication may be illuminated by an examination of these complications and the troubling issues they raise.

All begins with Amis and Amiloun, who are always at the center of the narrative surrounded by stock or token characters who exist and act only to illuminate the natures and behavior of the heroes. These "counters" are allowed only enough development to clarify the challenges that Amis and Amiloun face. The configurations of the heroes and the "counters" reveal the moral issues. It has been argued that the heroes begin and end at the same place. It does not seem to me, however, that characterization or character development is as important in the poem as the "problems" that they face, individually and together, in these changing configurations.

The first problem arises when they must separate. It is not problematic that they should be left by their parents in the service of "the duke." Such was a common practice in the Middle Ages and commonplace in romance. It only becomes intriguing by virtue of the simultaneity, their physical resemblance, and the bond that is thereby established. When Amiloun must return home to receive his lands upon the death of his parents, the possibilities for substantive problems emerge and are highlighted by the special attention the narrator gives to their parting:

> When thai were bothe afot light,   *on foot set*
> Sir Amiloun, that hendi knight,   *skillful*
> Was rightwise man of rede   *justly; counsel*
> And seyd to Sir Amis ful right,
> "Brother, as we er trewthe plight   *earlier pledged fidelity*
> Bothe with word and dede,
> Fro this day forward never mo
> To faile other for wele no wo,
> To help him at his nede,
> Brother, be now trewe to me,   *loyal*
> And y schal ben as trewe to the,
> Also God me spede!"   *God give me fortune*
>   (lines 289–300)

Without direct statement, the narrator makes us suspicious that distance will result in tests of the oath so prominently asserted and here reasserted. In the rest of his speech, Amiloun warns Amis of two potential problems which quickly materialize:

> "Ac brother, ich warn the biforn,   *But; I; in advance*
> For His love that bar the croun of thorn   *bore*
> To save al mankende,   *mankind*

Be nought ogain thi lord forsworn,	*in no way against your lord*
And yif thou dost, thou art forlorn	*if; lost*
Ever more withouten ende.	
Bot ever do trewthe and no tresoun	
And thenk on me, Sir Amiloun,	
Now we asondri schal wende.	*asunder shall travel*
And, brother, yete y the forbede	*still I warn you against*
The fals steward felawerede;	*fellowship*
Certes, he wil the schende!"	*destroy*

(lines 301–12)

While emphasizing their "brotherhood," Amiloun identifies precisely the difficulties Amis will immediately face. The steward is identified as evil even before he does anything evil, and the danger of infidelity to the duke is raised even before any temptation is offered to Amis.

Even without Amiloun's warning, readers of romance would expect a steward to be evil, and he quickly satisfies that expectation. He proposes a "trewthe-plight" with Amis as soon as Amiloun is gone. Amis rejects the offer on the grounds that, despite separation, his relationship with Amiloun is exclusive. Whatever the steward's motive, perhaps envy, Amis' reaction only serves to further antagonize the steward, against whom Amiloun has already warned him. There is a complex human problem in the steward's offer: jealous of the friendship of Amis and Amiloun, the steward is eager to replace Amiloun in Amis' favor. His attempt and Amis' rejection enrich the conventional and expectable treachery beyond simple jealousy without excusing his behavior. The steward begins jealous, seeks friendship, and in rejection becomes all the more bitter. This is a psychologically complex steward delineated in action rather than description or direct statement.

Amiloun's other warning, about fidelity to the duke, takes shape in the powerful passion that Belisaunt, the daughter of the duke, conceives for Amis. Here again the narrator complicates familiar conventions. That Belisaunt falls desperately in love with Amis just by looking at him and the oddity that she seems never to have seen him before should come as no surprise; love at first sight and unaccountable first sightings are common in romance. The complication is in that she turns out to be a "persistent wooer," a folklore motif grafted on to courtly love-longing and physical decline occasioned by a poignant encounter in a garden. She reveals her love and will not take no for an answer. She goes beyond the reticence of the courtly lady and even the calculated enticements of ladies like Bercilak's wife in *Sir Gawain and The Green Knight*. She presses her entreaty beyond the bounds not only of propriety but of morality. She threatens to cry rape if Amis does not acquiesce and coerces him into a profession of "love-plight." This is not a violation of his troth to Amiloun, but Amis makes it clear that it is a violation of his subordinate position and consequent duty as a member of the duke's household. Amis is trapped by Belisaunt's persistence and compromised by his own failure of nerve: he does the wrong thing and this is not a romance in which characters are protected from the moral consequences of their actions.

Belisaunt's successful stalking of Amis occurs while the duke is hunting, and he is finally seduced while the duke is hunting again. This is reminiscent of Sir Gawain's situation at the castle of Bercilak de Hautdesert, though in this case the literal hunter is unaware of the love-hunting going on at home. Although *Amis and Amiloun* lacks that complexity, it develops a complexity of its own by the way it rings changes on folk and romance conventions and capitalizes on the confluence of them. The evil, but correct, steward spies on the courtly, but culpable, rendezvous in Belisaunt's chamber. Despite Amis' misgivings, there is no doubt what happens:

And so thai plaid in word and dede,	*played*
That he wan hir maidenhede,	*won; maidenhead*
Er that sche went oway.	*Before; away*
(lines 766–68)	

When the narrator wishes to be clear he is perfectly clear. Initially, the evil steward has the moral high ground when he reports the transgression to the duke, regardless of his spiteful intention. The immediate consequence is the proposal of a trial by combat, yet another familiar circumstance but here fraught with paradox. The steward is evil, but in the right; Amis, however much he is a victim, is in the wrong and his compromised position is emphasized when he himself proposes the trial which, according to all that is right and good, he should not win. It is peculiar that the duke should so easily take the steward's word against Amis (and become so fierce and implacable), but it is appropriate that Amis have trouble finding "borwes" (guarantors) and have to rely on Belisaunt and her mother, the only two members of court who really do know his guilt. The complications of the moral universe are not only not ignored, but emphasized.

When Amis thinks of Amiloun as his only savior in the situation, he proceeds directly to seek his help despite the fact that the presentation of his moral situation makes it clear that he is abusing his "trewthe-plight" to save himself. The description of Amis' journey to Amiloun (his horse drops dead of fatigue and he continues on foot until he collapses) would in other circumstances be pathetic but here seems a sign of desperation, almost comic. Amiloun, on the other hand, becomes involved by having a conventional dream about the nearness of his friend and immediately acts on his vow of friendship. On the surface, his reaction is a conventional fidelity, but Amis' situation has become so compromised that it is hard to look on with a simple and sympathetic eye. When Amiloun sets out disguised as Amis so he can successfully defend the trial by combat, since his oath will technically be true, the established situation does not allow us to view the enterprise with the happy complicity we usually share in such "trick contests."

While Amiloun is off on his unworthy mission, Amis sleeps with Amiloun's wife. The fact that Amis ensures his chastity by placing a sword between Amiloun's wife and himself in bed is a convention of folklore and romance, but this narrator again shakes our sense of convention by having Amiloun's wife reflect on her "husband's" uncharacteristic sexual restraint in a comic and cranky way. This is a small point but illustrative of how the characters are not allowed the "reprieve of romance."

Meanwhile, Amiloun is engaging in a trial by combat which he and we know is a sham. The battle is intense and extended, a tour de force of the poet's narrative power, but we know all along that this is all wrong. When Amiloun wins, we are relieved; after all, the steward is a scoundrel and Amis was ensnared; but we are not reconciled. We cannot help but see the conflict in the context of Amis' dishonesty, Amiloun's prior warning, and the clear admonition that the angel gives to Amiloun before the battle:

. . . "Thou knight, Sir Amiloun,	
God, that suffred passioun,	
Sent the bode bi me;	*warning*
Yif thou this bataile underfong,	*undertake*

Thou schalt have an eventour strong   *adventure*
Within this yeres thre;
And or this thre yere be al gon,   *before*
Fouler mesel nas never non   *leper*
In the world, than thou schal be!"   (lines 1252–60)

And Amiloun explicitly rejects what is not only advice but reliable prediction:

"Certes," he seyd, "for drede of care
To hold mi treuthe schal y nought spare,
Lete God don alle His wille."   (lines 1282–84)

In keeping his word to Amis, Amiloun is directly challenging God. When Amis returns ostensibly vindicated, marries Belisaunt, and eventually inherits the kingdom, we cannot escape our sense that vice is its own reward — happily for Amis but disastrously for Amiloun who, within a year, contracts the promised leprosy, not only a physical visitation but, in medieval lore, a clear sign of moral culpability.

The unusual doubleness (or tripleness) of this narrative returns in Amiloun's wife's reaction to his affliction: she turns him out to a hut and eventually gives him an ass to travel with on the condition that he get out of the neighborhood for good. Her vindictiveness, even malignity, provides an interesting contrast, implied rather than specified, to Belisaunt's original amorality and her later generosity. So much for "token" wives. In any case, the result is that Amiloun must leave his home and wander as a beggar served only by the fair and faithful young Amoraunt. The steadfastness of Amoraunt's loyalty, through all of the touchingly described tribulations of Amiloun, cannot help but be seen in contrast with the relationship between Amiloun and Amis. There is no equal "plighting" here; Amoraunt simply serves Amiloun in a humble and determined way. Why Amiloun does not immediately seek out Amis for succor in his distress is not explained, but the fact that he does not allows Amoraunt to demonstrate a selfless and uncomplicated loyalty that is seen nowhere else in the poem. The description of his faithful service is long and edifying.

Through Amoraunt's good offices, Amiloun is recognized and received, joyfully and generously, by Amis and the now good Belisaunt. The key to the acceptance is, however, Amis' recognition of the cup, one of two identical cups Amiloun had made at the time of their original parting. Recognition through such a token is nothing new and in some ways fulfills our sense of the rightness of the resolution, but the narrator will not leave well enough alone. Amiloun still must be healed of his leprosy (in the logic of this poem) and this procedure occasions still further moral ambiguities.

Amis has a dream in which he is told that Amiloun will be cured only if Amis kills his two children and anoints Amiloun with their blood. Amis agonizes over his dilemma but really he has no choice. He expresses his anguish, does the deed, and Amiloun is healed. Now, I have expressed this sequence of events flatly and without moral excuses, because that is the effect of the way the narrator tells the story. It is difficult by this time to have unambiguous sympathy with Amis' plight. His anguish is pathetic, but his behavior is already determined by the ambiguous logic of the poem. Everything is now resolved, except of course Amis has slaughtered his children. The description of his behavior once again does not allow him the "reprieve of romance." There is, however, another resolution, derived from saints' legends but used here in a darker context: the children are, miraculously, found alive and well. In other circumstances, this could be accepted as hagiographic, a "miracle of the Virgin" or the intervention of some patron saint. But the world is already too messy for easy acceptance of this resolution as praise of God for intervening on behalf of a larger good. Too much has gone wrong in this world for us to find pleasure in divine vindication. Rather, the preservation (resurrection?) of the children simply provides an assertively happy ending, which, as I have indicated before, the tendency of the narrative has not earned. The consequence is that there is an irony in the resolution which, although it does not damn Amis or Amiloun or Belisaunt, will not let us forget the unresolved moral ambiguities of the tale.

By looking only at results, *Amis and Amiloun* can be seen as a simple vindication of the value of friendship, or "trewthe," in the face of imposing challenges. The problem is that the story is not told that way. We are continually asked to see complexities and to remember them. In this implacability, we are reminded of comparable examples of moral ambiguity in the late fourteenth and early fifteenth century: Gawain's self-doubt despite his comrades' approbation in *Sir Gawain and the Green Knight*, Lancelot's attractiveness despite his culpability in the *Stanzaic Morte Arthur* and Malory. In *Amis and Amiloun*, romance conventions are configured so as to call into question the possibility, even the propriety, of total devotion to an abstraction: *Amis and Amiloun* fits a pattern that signals if not the end of idealism at least a hearty skepticism about its efficacy. Chaucer was not alone in his critique of local ethics. Lillian Herlands Hornstein (in J. Burke Severs' *A Manual of the Writings in Middle English*) is correct to classify the poem among the romances of "Didactic Intent," but the didacticism of *Amis and Amiloun* reveals a world of moral ambiguity and tenuous ideals.

Select Bibliography

Manuscripts

Advocates 19.2.1 (Auchinleck), at the National Library of Scotland, Edinburgh. Fols. 49r–61v. [c. 1330. 2287 lines, missing beginning and ending. The base text for this edition.]

BM Egerton 2862 (formerly Trentham-Sutherland), at the British Library, London. Fols. 135r–147v. [c. 1400. 2186 lines, supplying a trustworthy version of the beginning and ending.]

Bodleian 21900 (Douce 326), at the Bodleian Library, Oxford University. Fols. 1r–13v. [c. 1500. 293 lines, often faulty.]

BM Harley 2386, at the British Library, London. Fols. 131r–137v. [c. 1500. A fragment of 894 lines.]

Previous Editions

The Auchinleck Manuscript. National Library of Scotland Advocates' MS 19.2.1. With an introduction by Derek Pearsall and I. C. Cunningham. London: The Scolar Press, 1979.

Fellows, Jennifer. *Of Love and Chivalry: An Anthology of Middle English Romance*. Everyman's Library. London: Charles E. Tuttle, 1993. Pp. 73–145.

Kölbing, Eugen, ed. *Amis and Amiloun, zugleich mit der altfranzösischen Quelle*. Altenglische Biblioteck 2. Heilbronn: Henninger, 1884.

Leach, MacEdward, ed. *Amis and Amiloun*. EETS o.s. 203. London: Oxford University Press, 1937. Reprinted 1960.

Le Saux, Françoise, ed. *Amys and Amylion*. Exeter: University of Exeter Press, 1993. [Based on the Bodleian (Douce) MS.]

Rickert, Edith. *Early English Romances in Verse*. New York: Cooper Square Publishers, 1967. [Modernized text.]

Weber, Henry. ed. *Metrical Romances of the Thirteenth, Fourteenth, and Fifteenth Centuries*. 3 vols. Edinburgh: George Ramsay and Company, 1810. Vol. 2. Pp. 367–473. [Uses Auchinleck as his base text with the beginning and ending taken from the Bodleian (Douce) MS.]

Criticism

Baldwin, Dean R. "*Amis and Amiloun*: The Testing of Treuthe." *Papers on Language and Literature* 16 (1980), 353–65.

Cook, Robert G. "Chaucer's Pandarus and the Medieval Ideal of Friendship." *JEGP* 69 (1970), 407–24.

Dannenbaum, Susan. "Insular Tradition in the Story of Amis and Amiloun." *Neophilologus* 67 (1983), 611–22.

Delany, Sheila. "A, A, and B: Coding Same-Sex Union in *Amis and Amiloun*." *Pulp Fictions of Medieval England*. Ed. Nicola McDonald. Manchester: Manchester University Press, 2004. Pp. 63–81.

Fewster, C. S. *Narrative Transformations of Past and Present in Middle English Romance: Guy of Warwick, Amis and Amiloun, and the Squyr of Lowe Degre*. Liverpool: University of Liverpool, 1984.

Ford, John C. "Merry Married Brothers: Wedded Friendship, Lovers' Language and Male Matrimonials in Two Middle English Romances." *Medieval Forum* 3 (2003). http://www.sfsu.edu/~medieval/Volume3/Brothers.html.

———. "Contrasting the Identical: Differentiation of the 'Indistinguishable' Characters of *Amis and Amiloun*." *Neophilologus* 86 (2002), 311–23.

———. "A New Conception of Poetic Formulae Based on Prototype Theory and the Mental Template." *Neuphilologishche Mitteilungen* 103 (2002), 205–26.

Heather, P. J. "Sworn-Brotherhood." *Folklore* 63 (1952), 158–72.

Hume, Kathryn. "*Amis and Amiloun* and the Aesthetics of Middle English Romance." *Studies in Philology* 70 (1973), 19–41.

Johnston, Alexandra F. "'Amys and Amylon' at Bicester Priory." *Records of Early English Drama Newsletter* 18.2 (1993), 15–18.

Jost, Jean E. "Hearing the Female Voice: Transgression in *Amis and Amiloun*." *Medieval Perspectives* 10 (1995), 116–32.

Kramer, Dale. "Structural Artistry in *Amis and Amiloun*." *Annuale Mediaevale* 9 (1968), 103–22.

Kratins, Ojars. "The Middle English *Amis and Amiloun*: Chivalric Romance or Secular Hagiography." *PMLA* 81 (1966), 347–54.

Mehl, Dieter. *The Middle English Romances of the Thirteenth and Fourteenth Centuries*. London: Routledge & Kegan Paul, 1968 [1969].

For Goddes love in Trinyté	
Al that ben hend herkenith to me,	*are courteous listen*
I pray yow, par amoure,	*by (the) love (of God)*
What sumtyme fel beyond the see	*once upon a time happened*
5 Of two Barons of grete bounté	*Concerning; generosity*
And men of grete honoure;	
Her faders were barons hende,	*Their fathers; well-born*
Lordinges com of grete kynde	*Lords born of great family*
And pris men in toun and toure;	*excellent; town and tower*
10 To here of these children two	*hear*
How they were in wele and woo,	*good and ill*
Ywys, it is grete doloure.	*Certainly; sorrow*
In weele and woo how they gan wynd	*good and ill; fared*
And how unkouth they were of kynd,	*unaffected by their lineage*
15 The children bold of chere,	*manner*
And how they were good and hend	*courteous*
And how yong thei becom frend	*became friends*
In cort there they were,	*court where*
And how they were made knyght	*knighted*
20 And how they were trouth plyght,	*how they pledged loyalty*
The children both in fere,	*together*
And in what lond thei were born	
And what the childres name worn,	*children's names were*
Herkeneth and ye mow here.	*Listen; will hear*
25 In Lumbardy, y understond,	
Whilom bifel in that lond,	*Once upon a time it happened*
In romance as we reede,	*read*
Two barouns hend wonyd in lond	*barons well-born lived*
And had two ladyes free to fond,	*noble in proof*
30 That worthy were in wede;	*stately were in dress*
Of her hend ladyes two	*their well-born*
Twoo knave childre gat they thoo	*Two boy children got they then*
That douhty were of dede,	*doughty (brave)*
And trew weren in al thing,	*true (to their word)*

35	And therfore Jhesu, hevynking,	*king of heaven*
	Ful wel quyted her mede.	*fulfilled their deserving*

	The childrenis names, as y yow hyght,	*children's; as I promised you*
	In ryme y wol rekene ryght	*will recount properly*
	And tel in my talkyng;	
40	Both they were getyn in oo nyght	*conceived; one*
	And on oo day born aplyght,	*one; truly*
	For soth, without lesyng;	*Truthfully, without lying*
	That oon baroun son, ywys	*one; certainly*
	Was ycleped childe Amys	*named*
45	At his cristenyng;	*baptism*
	That other was clepyd Amylyoun,	*named*
	That was a childe of grete renoun	*renown*
	And com of hyghe ofspryng.	*high background*

	The children gon then thryve,	*then began to thrive*
50	Fairer were never noon on lyve,	*none alive*
	Curtaise, hende, and good;	*Courteous, well-born*
	When they were of yeres fyve,	*five years old*
	Alle her kyn was of hem blyth,	*family; pleased*
	So mylde they were of mood;	*mild; manner*
55	When they were sevyn yere olde,	
	Grete joy every man of hem tolde	
	To beholde that frely foode;	*worthy offspring*
	When they were twel winter olde,	*twelve*
	In al the londe was ther non hold	*held*
60	So faire of boon and blood.	*bone and blood (i.e., body)*

	In that tyme, y understond,	
	A duk wonyd in that lond,	*duke lived*
	Prys in toun and toure;	*Esteemed in town and tower*
	Frely he let sende his sonde,	*Graciously he sent his message*
65	After Erles, Barouns, fre and bond,	*To earls, barons, freemen and bound*
	And ladies bryght in boure;	*lovely; bower*
	A ryche fest he wolde make	*rich feast*
	Al for Jhesu Cristes sake	
	That is oure savyoure;	*savior*
70	Muche folk, as y yow saye,	*as I tell you*
	He lete after sende that daye	*He invited*
	With myrth and grete honoure.	*With joy*

	Thoo Barouns twoo, that y of tolde,	*Those*
	And her sones feire and bolde	*fair*
75	To court they com ful yare.	*quickly*
	When they were samned, yong and olde,	*gathered*
	Mony men gan hem byholde	*looked at them*

Of lordynges that there were,
Of body how wel they were pyght,   *adorned*
80   And how feire they were of syght,   *fair they were to see*
Of hyde and hew and here;   *skin; complexion; hair*
And al they seide without lesse   *falsehood*
Fairer children than they wesse   *were*
Ne sey they never yere.   *They never saw before*

85   In al the court was ther no wyght,   *person*
Erl, baroun, squyer, ne knyght,   *Earl, baron, squire, nor knight*
Neither lef ne loothe,   *Like it or not*
So lyche they were both of syght   *alike; appearance*
And of waxing, y yow plyght,   *stature; pledge*
90   I tel yow for soothe,   *truly*
In al thing they were so lyche   *alike*
Ther was neither pore ne ryche,   *poor nor rich*
Who so beheld hem both,
Fader ne moder that couth say   *Father nor mother that could say*
95   Ne knew the hend children tway   *Nor could tell the courteous children apart*
But by the coloure of her cloth.   *Except; clothes*

That riche douke his fest gan hold   *duke*
With erles and with barouns bold,   *earls; barons*
As ye may listen and lithe,   *hear*
100   Fourtennight, as me was told,   *Fortnight (two weeks)*
With meet and drynke, meryst on mold   *merriest on earth*
To glad the bernes blithe;   *cheer; noblemen joyful*
Ther was mirthe and melodye
And al maner of menstracie   *minstrelsy*
105   Her craftes for to kithe;   *Their skills; show*
Opon the fiftenday ful yare   *quite readily*
Thai token her leve forto fare   *They took leave to go*
And thonked him mani a sithe.   *many a time*

Than the lordinges schuld forth wende,   *When; lords; left*
110   That riche douke comly of kende   *noble of family*
Cleped to him that tide   *Called to him then*
Tho tuay barouns, that were so hende,   *Those two baron; courteous*
And prayd hem also his frende   *entreated them as*
In court thai schuld abide,
115   And lete her tuay sones fre   *splendid*
In his servise with him to be,
Semly to fare bi his side;   *In fine array to live by*
And he wald dubbe hem knightes to   *would dub them*
And susten hem for ever mo,   *support*
120   As lordinges proude in pride.   *lords magnificent in honor*

	The riche barouns answerd ogain,	*in return*
	And her levedis gan to sain	*their ladies began to say*
	To that douke ful yare	*quite readily*
	That thai were bothe glad and fain	*joyful*
125	That her levely children tuain	*their dear; both*
	In servise with him ware.	*were*
	Thai gave her childer her blisceing	*their children their blessing*
	And bisought Jhesu, heven king,	
	He schuld scheld hem fro care,	*would shield them from grief*
130	And oft thai thonked the douke that day	*frequently thanked the duke*
	And token her leve and went oway	*took their leave; away*
	To her owen contres thai gun fare.	*To their own countries they began to travel*
	Thus war tho hende childer, ywis,	*those lovely; certainly*
	Child Amiloun and child Amis,	
135	In court frely to fede,	*freely to eat (be nourished)*
	To ride an hunting under riis;	*branches*
	Over al the lond than were thai priis	*then; esteemed*
	And worthliest in wede.	*worthiest in clothes*
	So wele tho children loved hem tho,	*well; loved each other then*
140	Nas never children loved hem so,	*Never did children love each other so*
	Noither in word no in dede;	*Neither in word nor in deed*
	Bituix hem tuai, of blod and bon,	*Between them two, of blood and bone*
	Trewer love nas never non,	*There was never truer love*
	In gest as so we rede.	*stories; read*
145	On a day the childer, war and wight,	*alert and brave*
	Trewethes togider thai gun plight,	*Pledged their loyalty together*
	While thai might live and stond	
	That bothe bi day and bi night,	*by*
	In wele and wo, in wrong and right,	*good and ill*
150	That thai schuld frely fond	*nobly try*
	To hold togider at everi nede,	*to stick together*
	In word, in werk, in wille, in dede,	
	Where that thai were in lond,	*Wherever*
	Fro that day forward never mo	
155	Failen other for wele no wo:	*Let each other down*
	Therto thai held up her hond.	*(i.e., swore an oath)*
	Thus in gest as ye may here,	*stories; hear*
	Tho hende childer in cuntré were	*Those courteous*
	With that douke for to abide;	
160	The douke was blithe and glad of chere,	*happy; manner*
	Thai were him bothe leve and dere,	*beloved and dear*
	Semly to fare bi his side.	*Honorably to go by*
	Tho thai were fiften winter old,	*When*
	He dubbed bothe tho bernes bold	*brave young men*

165   To knightes in that tide,   *To be; time*

        And fond hem al that hem was nede,   *gave them all that was necessary for them*

        Hors and wepen and worthly wede,   *weapons; arms*

        As princes prout in pride.   *proud*

         That riche douke, he loved hem so,

170   Al that thai wald he fond hem tho,   *He provided them all they wanted*

        Bothe stedes white and broun,   *horses*

        That in what stede thai gun go,   *So that; places; went*

        Alle the lond spac of hem tho,   *spoke; then*

        Bothe in tour and toun;

175   In to what stede that thai went,   *place*

        To justes other to turnament,   *To jousts or to tournaments*

        Sir Amis and Sir Amiloun,

        For douhtiest in everi dede,   *As doughtiest; deed*

        With scheld and spere to ride on stede,   *horse*

180   Thai gat hem gret renoun.

         That riche douke hadde of hem pris,   *esteem*

        For that thai were so war and wiis   *alert and wise*

        And holden of gret bounté.   *generosity*

        Sir Amiloun and Sir Amis,

185   He sett hem bothe in gret office,   *them; high*

        In his court for to be;

        Sir Amis, as ye may here,   *you; hear*

        He made his chef botelere,   *head dispenser (of food and drink)*

        For he was hend and fre,   *courteous and generous*

190   And Sir Amiloun of hem alle   *over them all*

        He made chef steward in halle,   *manager of domestic affairs*

        To dight al his meine.   *To set in order all members of his household*

         In to her servise when thai were brought,   *their*

        To geten hem los tham spared nought, *To earn themselves praise; spared nothing*

195   Wel hendeliche thai bigan;   *honorably*

        With riche and pover so wele thai wrought,   *poor so well they behaved*

        Al that hem seighe, with word and thought,   *them saw*

        Hem loved mani a man;   *Many a man loved them*

        For thai were so blithe of chere,   *graceful of manner*

200   Over al the lond fer and nere   *far and near*

        The los of love thai wan,   *honor*

        And the riche douke, withouten les,   *lies*

        Of all the men that olive wes   *alive were*

        Mest he loved hem than.   *Most he loved them then*

205   Than hadde the douke, ich understond,   *I*

        A chef steward of alle his lond,   *manager of property*

        A douhti knight at crie,   *doughty; upon call*

That ever he proved with nithe and ond   *tried with envy and indignation*
For to have brought hem bothe to schond   *To bring them both to shame*
210   With gile and trecherie.   *guile*
For thai were so gode and hende,
And for the douke was so wele her frende,   *because; friend*
He hadde therof gret envie;
To the douke with wordes grame   *harmful*
215   Ever he proved to don hem schame   *tried to do them shame*
With wel gret felonie.   *crime*

So within tho yeres to   *So then within two years*
A messanger ther com tho   *there*
To Sir Amiloun, hende on hond,   *skillful with hands*
220   And seyd hou deth hadde fet him fro   *And said how death had fetched from him*
His fader and his moder also   *father; mother*
Thurch the grace of Godes sond.   *Through; mercy*
Than was that knight a careful man,   *sorrowful*
To that douke he went him than
225   And dede him to understond   *explained to him*
His fader and his moder hende   *gracious*
War ded, and he most hom wende,   *go*
For to resaive his lond.   *receive (claim)*

That riche douke, comly of kende,   *noble of family*
230   Answerd ogain with wordes hende   *in return*
And seyd, "So God me spede,   *God give me fortune*
Sir Amiloun, now thou schalt wende   *go*
Me nas never so wo for frende   *I was never so sorry*
That of mi court out yede.   *That out of my; went*
235   Ac yif ever it befalle so   *But if; happens*
That thou art in wer and wo   *danger and sorrow*
And of min help hast nede,
Saveliche com or send thi sond,   *Only; messenger*
And with al mi powere of mi lond
240   Y schal wreke the of that dede."   *avenge*

Than was Sir Amiloun ferli wo   *terribly sorry*
For to wende Sir Amis fro,   *go; from*
On him was al his thought.
To a goldsmithe he gan go   *went*
245   And lete make gold coupes to,   *had made; cups two*
For thre hundred pounde he hem bought,   *them*
That bothe were of o wight,   *one (the same) weight*
And bothe of o michel, yplight;   *one (the same) size, truly*
Ful richeliche thai were wrought,   *richly*
250   And bothe thai weren as liche, ywis,   *alike*

As was Sir Amiloun and Sir Amis,
Ther no failed right nought.   *Nothing went wrong with that*

 When that Sir Amiloun was al yare,   *ready*
He tok his leve for to fare,   *travel*
255 To wende in his jorné.   *go; journey*
Sir Amis was so ful of care,
For sorwe and wo and sikeing sare,   *sorrow; woe; sighing sadly*
Almost swoned that fre.   *Almost fainted; nobleman*
To the douke he went with dreri mode   *sorrowful manner*
260 And praid him fair, ther he stode,   *prayed; where*
And seyd, "Sir, par charité,   *for charity*
Yif me leve to wend the fro,   *Give me leave to travel from you*
Bot yif y may with mi brother go,   *Unless*
Mine hert, it breketh of thre!"   *in three*

265 That riche douke, comly of kende,   *noble of family*
Answerd ogain with wordes hende   *in return*
And seyd withouten delay,
"Sir Amis, mi gode frende,
Wold ye bothe now fro me wende?"
270 "Certes," he seyd, "nay!
Were ye bothe went me fro,   *gone from me*
Than schuld me waken al mi wo,
Mi joie were went oway.   *would be gone away*
Thi brother schal in to his cuntré;   *country*
275 Wende with him in his jurné   *Go; journey*
And com ogain this day!"   *back*

 When thai were redi forto ride,
Tho bold bernes for to abide   *Those; young men*
Busked hem redy boun.   *Prepared; to go forth*
280 Hende, herkneth! Is nought to hide,   *Gracious audience, listen*
So douhti knightes, in that tide   *Such doughty; time*
That ferd out of that toun,   *traveled*
Al that day as thai rade   *rode*
Gret morning bothe thai made,   *mourning*
285 Sir Amis and Amiloun,
And when thai schuld wende otuain,   *go apart (separate)*
Wel fair togider opon a plain   *together on*
Of hors thai light adoun.   *They got off their horses*

 When thai were bothe afot light,   *on foot set*
290 Sir Amiloun, that hendi knight,   *skillful*
Was rightwise man of rede   *justly; counsel*
And seyd to Sir Amis ful right,
"Brother, as we er trewthe plight   *earlier pledged fidelity*

Bothe with word and dede,
295   Fro this day forward never mo
To faile other for wele no wo,
To help him at his nede,
Brother, be now trewe to me,   *loyal*
And y schal ben as trewe to the,
300   Also God me spede!   *God give me fortune*

Ac brother, ich warn the biforn,   *But; I; in advance*
For His love that bar the croun of thorn   *bore*
To save al mankende,   *mankind*
Be nought ogain thi lord forsworn,   *in no way against your lord*
305   And yif thou dost, thou art forlorn   *if; lost*
Ever more withouten ende.
Bot ever do trewthe and no tresoun
And thenk on me, Sir Amiloun,
Now we asondri schal wende.   *asunder shall travel*
310   And, brother, yete y the forbede   *still I warn you against*
The fals steward felawerede;   *fellowship*
Certes, he wil the schende!"   *destroy*

As thai stode so, tho bretheren bold,   *stood; brothers*
Sir Amiloun drought forth tuay coupes of gold,   *draw; two cups*
315   Ware liche in al thing,   *[Which] were alike*
And bad sir Amis that he schold   *bade*
Chese whether he have wold,   *Choose which he would have*
Withouten more duelling,   *delay*
And seyd to him, "Mi leve brother,   *dear*
320   Kepe thou that on and y that other,   *one*
For Godes love, heven king;
Lete never this coupe fro the,   *Let*
Bot loke heron and thenk on me,   *here on*
It tokneth our parting."   *betokens*

325   Gret sorwe thai made at her parting   *Great sorrow; their*
And kisten hem with eighen wepeing,   *kissed; eyes weeping*
Tho knightes hende and fre.
Aither bitaught other heven king,   *Each commended the other to*
And on her stedes thai gun spring   *horses; mounted*
330   And went in her jurné.   *their journeys*
Sir Amiloun went hom to his lond
And sesed it al in to his hond,   *took*
That his elders hadde be,   *That his ancestors had held*
And spoused a levedy bright in bour   *espoused; lady beautiful; bower*
335   And brought hir hom with gret honour   *her home*
And miche solempneté.   *much solemnity*

	Lete we Sir Amiloun stille be	*Let*
	With his wiif in his cuntré —	*wife; country*
	God leve hem wele to fare —	*grant*
340	And of Sir Amis telle we;	
	When he com hom to court oye,	*again*
	Ful blithe of him thai ware;	*glad*
	For that he was so hende and gode,	*gracious*
	Men blisced him, bothe bon and blod,	*blessed; bone and blood (body)*
345	That ever him gat and bare,	*Who ever conceived and bore him*
	Save the steward of that lond;	*Except*
	Ever he proved with nithe and ond	*Always; tried; malice and anger*
	To bring him into care.	*grief*

	Than on a day bifel it so	*it happened*
350	With the steward he met tho,	*then*
	Ful fair he gret that fre.	*greeted; noble person*
	"Sir Amis," he seyd, "the is ful wo	*you are woeful*
	For that thi brother is went the fro,	*Because; from*
	And, certes, so is me.	*certainly so am I*
355	Ac of his wendeing have thou no care,	*But; going*
	Yif thou wilt leve opon mi lare,	*If; believe; teaching*
	And lete thi morning be,	*leave off your mourning*
	And thou wil be to me kende,	*If; of one kind (kin)*
	Y schal the be a better frende	
360	Than ever yete was he.	

	"Sir Amis," he seyd, "do bi mi red,	*act on my advice*
	And swere ous bothe brotherhed	*us; brotherhood*
	And plight we our trewthes to;	*pledge; fidelity*
	Be trewe to me in word and dede,	
365	And y schal to the, so God me spede,	*to you*
	Be trewe to the also."	
	Sir Amis answerd, "Mi treuthe y plight	*pledged*
	To Sir Amiloun, the gentil knight,	
	Thei he be went me fro.	*Though*
370	Whiles that y may gon and speke,	*walk and speak*
	Y no schal never mi treuthe breke,	*break*
	Noither for wele no wo.	*Neither*

	For bi the treuthe that God me sende,	*truth*
	Ichave him founde so gode and kende,	*I have; kind (good-natured)*
375	Seththen that y first him knewe,	*Since*
	For ones y plight him treuthe, that hende,	*once I pledged; courteous one*
	Where so he in warld wende,	*world should go*
	Y schal be to him trewe;	
	And yif y were now forsworn	*if*
380	And breke mi treuthe, y were forlorn,	*broke; vow; totally lost*

Wel sore it schuld me rewe.   *grievously; rue*
Gete me frendes whare y may,   *Get; friends where*
Y no schal never bi night no day
Chaunge him for no newe."   *Exchange*

385   The steward than was egre of mode,   *fierce of manner*
Almest for wrethe he wex ner wode   *Almost for wrath he grew near mad*
And seyd, withouten delay,
And swore bi Him that dyed on Rode: *died on the Cross*
"Thou traitour, unkinde blod,   *unnatural of breeding*
390   Thou schalt abigge this nay.   *atone for this refusal*
Y warn the wele," he seyd than,
"That y schal be thi strong foman   *enemy*
Ever after this day!"
Sir Amis answerd tho,   *then*
395   "Sir, therof give y nought a slo;   *I don't give a fig*
Do al that thou may!"

Al thus the wrake gan biginne,   *trouble did begin*
And with wrethe thai went atuinne,   *wrath; apart*
Tho bold bernes to.   *Those bold young men two*
400   The steward nold never blinne   *would never cease*
To schende that douhti knight of kinne,   *shame*
Ever he proved tho.   *Always he tried thus*
Thus in court togider thai were   *together*
With wrethe and with loureand chere   *wrath; surly face*
405   Wele half a yere and mo,   *more*
And afterward opon a while
The steward with tresoun and gile   *guile*
Wrought him ful michel wo.   *great sorrow*

So in a time, as we tel in gest,   *stories*
410   The riche douke lete make a fest   *put on a feast*
Semly in somers tide;   *Properly; time*
Ther was mani a gentil gest   *guest*
With mete and drink ful onest   *meat; most fitting*
To servi by ich a side.   *serve all around*
415   Miche semly folk was samned thare,   *Many worthy; gathered*
Erls, barouns, lasse and mare,   *lesser and greater*
And levedis proude in pride.   *ladies magnificent in honor*
More joie no might be non
Than ther was in that worthly won,   *worthy dwelling*
420   With blisse in borwe to bide.   *castle to abide*

That riche douke, that y of told,
He hadde a douhter fair and bold,   *daughter*
Curteise, hende and fre.   *lovely and generous*

When sche was fiften winter old,

425   In al that lond nas ther non yhold   *there was none held*

So semly on to se,   *So splendid to look at*

For sche was gentil and avenaunt,   *noble; beautiful*

Hir name was cleped Belisaunt,   *called*

As ye may lithe at me.   *listen to*

430   With levedis and maidens bright in bour *ladies; beautiful in bower*

Kept sche was with honour

And gret solempnité.   *solemnity*

    That fest lasted fourten night   *feast*

Of barouns and of birddes bright   *ladies beautiful*

435   And lordinges mani and fale.   *lords many and abundant*

Ther was mani a gentil knight

And mani a serjaunt, wise and wight,   *servant; strong*

To serve tho hende in halle.   *those nobles in hall*

Than was the boteler, Sir Amis,   *chief dispenser*

440   Over al yholden flour and priis,   *held flower and prize*

Trewely to telle in tale,

And douhtiest in everi dede

And worthliest in ich a wede   *all his clothes*

And semliest in sale.   *most splendid in the hall*

445   Than the lordinges schulden al gon   *all had to go*

And wende out of that worthli won,   *traveled; dwelling*

In boke as so we rede,

That mirie maide gan aske anon   *lovely*

Of her maidens everichon   *every one*

450   And seyd, "So God you spede,   *God give you fortune*

Who was hold the doughtiest knight   *considered*

And semlyest in ich a sight   *most splendid in every view*

And worthliest in wede,   *worthiest in dress*

And who was the fairest man

455   That was yholden in lond than,   *considered; then*

And doughtiest of dede?"

    Her maidens gan answere ogain   *began; in return*

And seyd, "Madame, we schul the sain   *shall to you say*

That sothe bi Seyn Savour: *truth; Holy Savior*

460   Of erls, barouns, knight and swain   *young men*

The fairest man and mest of main   *most of force*

And man of mest honour,   *most*

It is Sir Amis, the kinges boteler;   *chief dispenser*

In al this warld nis his per,   *world is not his peer*

465   Noither in toun no tour;   *Neither*

He is douhtiest in dede

And worthliest in everi wede   *worthiest; armor*
And chosen for priis and flour."   *prize and flower*

Belisaunt, that birdde bright,   *lady beautiful*
470   When thai hadde thus seyd, yplight,   *truly*
As ye may listen and lithe,   *hear*
On Sir Amis, that gentil knight,
Ywis, hir love was al alight,   *Indeed; kindled*
That no man might it kithe.   *realize*
475   Wher that sche seighe him ride or go,   *Wherever; saw; ride or walk*
Hir thought hir hert brac atuo,   *She; heart would break in two*
That hye no spac nought with that blithe;   *she never spoke; graceful one*
For hye no might night no day   *Because she*
Speke with him, that fair may,   *maiden*
480   Sche wepe wel mani a sithe.   *wept; many a time*

Thus that miri maiden ying   *merry; young*
Lay in care and lovemorning   *sorrow; love-mourning*
Bothe bi night and day;
As y you tel in mi talking,
485   For sorwe sche spac with him no thing,   *spoke*
Sike in bed sche lay.   *Ill*
Hir moder com to hir tho   *mother; then*
And gan to frain hir of hir wo,   *ask*
Help hir yif hye may;   *if she*
490   And sche answerd withouten wrong,
Hir pines were so hard and strong,   *pains*
Sche wald be loken in clay.   *wanted to be locked in clay (buried)*

That riche douke in o morning   *on one*
And with him mani a gret lording,   *great lord*
495   As prince prout in pride,
Thai dight him withouten dueling,   *prepared themselves; delay*
For to wende on dere hunting,   *go*
And busked hem for to ride.   *dressed themselves*
When the lordinges everichon   *lords everyone*
500   Were went out of that worthli won —   *stately residence*
In herd is nought to hide —   *In a crowd*
Sir Amis, withouten les,   *lies*
For a malady that on him wes,   *was*
At hom he gan to abide.   *stayed*

505   When tho lordinges were out ywent   *those lords*
With her men hende and bowes bent,   *skillful; bows*
To hunte on holtes hare,   *deep woods*
Than Sir Amis, verrament,   *truly*
He bileft at hom in present,   *stayed*

510	To kepe al that ther ware.	*attend to*
	That hendi knight bithought him tho,	*courteous; thought to himself then*
	Into the gardin he wold go,	
	For to solas him thare.	*solace himself there*
	Under a bough as he gan bide,	
515	To here the foules song that tide,	*birds'; time*
	Him thought a blisseful fare.	*state*

Now, hende, herkneth, and ye may here *gracious audience, listen*
Hou that the doukes douhter dere
Sike in hir bed lay. *Ill*
520 Hir moder com with diolful chere *doleful countenance*
And al the levedis that ther were, *ladies*
For to solas that may: *comfort; maiden*
"Arise up," sche seyd, "douhter min, *mine*
And go play the in to the gardin
525 This semly somers day; *lovely summer's*
Ther may thou here the foules song *hear*
With joie and miche blis among, *much*
Thi care schal wende oway." *go away*

Up hir ros that swete wight. *creature*
530 Into the gardine sche went ful right
With maidens hende and fre.
The somers day was fair and bright, *summer's*
The sonne him schon thurch lem of light, *shone through gleaming*
That semly was on to se. *splendid*
535 Sche herd the foules gret and smale, *birds*
The swete note of the nightingale
Ful mirily sing on tre; *merrily; tree*
Ac hir hert was so hard ibrought, *But her heart; troubled*
On love-longing was al hir thought,
540 No might hir gamen no gle. *She could not play or enjoy*

And so that mirie may with pride *merry maiden*
Went into the orchard that tide, *time*
To slake hir of hir care. *relieve*
Than seyghe sche Sir Amis biside, *saw; nearby*
545 Under a bough he gan abide, *remained*
To here tho mirthes mare. *that sweet singing better*
Than was sche bothe glad and blithe, *glad and joyful*
Hir joie couthe sche noman kithe, *could she no one show*
When that sche seighe him thare; *saw*
550 And thought sche wold for noman wond *no one hesitate*
That sche no wold to him fond *make her way*
And tel him of hir fare. *state*

	Than was that may so blithe o mode,	*maiden so happy of mood*
	When sche seighe were he stode,	*saw where he stood*
555	To him sche went, that swete,	*lovely one*
	And thought, for alle this warldes gode,	*world's possessions*
	Bot yif hye spac that frely fode,	*Until she spoke to that noble young man*
	That time no wold sche lete.	*let pass*
	And as tite as that gentil knight	*soon*
560	Seighe that bird in bour so bright	*Saw; woman; bower; beautiful*
	Com with him for to mete,	*Came towards him to meet*
	Ogaines hir he gan wende,	*Towards*
	With worde bothe fre and hende	
	Ful fair he gan hir grete.	*greet*

565	That mirie maiden sone anon	*immediately*
	Bad hir maidens fram hir gon	*Bade*
	And withdrawe hem oway;	*away*
	And when thai were togider alon,	*together alone*
	To Sir Amis sche made hir mon	*plea*
570	And seyd opon hir play,	*in her courtly love talk*
	"Sir knight, on the mine hert is brought,	*on you my heart*
	The to love is al mi thought	
	Bothe bi night and day;	
	That bot thou wolt mi leman be,	*unless; beloved*
575	Ywis, min hert breketh a thre,	*Certainly; in three*
	No lenger libben y no may.	*live*

	"Thou art," sche seyd, "a gentil knight,	*noble*
	And icham a bird in bour bright,	*I am a woman*
	Of wel heighe kin ycorn,	*From noble family descended*
580	And bothe bi day and bi night	
	Mine hert so hard is on the light,	*descended*
	Mi joie is al forlorn;	
	Plight me thi trewthe thou schalt be trewe	*Pledge; fidelity*
	And chaunge me for no newe	*exchange; no new (other)*
585	That in this world is born,	
	And y plight the mi treuthe also,	*pledge; fidelity*
	Til God and deth dele ous ato,	*set us apart*
	Y schal never be forsworn."	*break my vow*

	That hende knight stille he stode	
590	And al for thought chaunged his mode	*manner*
	And seyd with hert fre,	*generous*
	"Madame, for Him that dyed on Rode,	*died on the Cross*
	Astow art comen of gentil blode	*As you; noble*
	And air of this lond schal be,	*heir*
595	Bithenke the of thi michel honour;	*Remember; great*
	Kinges sones and emperour	

Nar non to gode to the; *Are none too good for you*
Certes, than were it michel unright, *much*
Thi love to lain opon a knight *lay*
600 That nath noither lond no fe. *has neither property nor rents*

"And yif we schuld that game biginne, *if; love game*
And ani wight of al thi kinne *person; family*
Might it undergo, *find out*
Al our joie and worldes winne *pleasure*
605 We schuld lese, and for that sinne *lose*
Wrethi God therto. *Anger; thereby*
And y dede mi lord this deshonour, *If*
Than were ich an ivel traitour; *evil*
Ywis, it may nought be so. *Certainly*
610 Leve madame, do bi mi red *Dear; advice*
And thenk what wil com of this dede:
Certes, no thing bot wo." *but woe*

That mirie maiden of gret renoun *lovely maiden*
Answerd, "Sir knight, thou nast no croun; *have no tonsure*
615 For God that bought the dere, *redeemed you dearly*
Whether artow prest other persoun, *Are you a priest or parson*
Other thou art monk other canoun, *Or; canon*
That prechest me thus here? *preaches*
Thou no schust have ben no knight, *should*
620 To gon among maidens bright,
Thou schust have ben a frere! *should; friar*
He that lerd the thus to preche, *taught you; preach*
The devel of helle ichim biteche, *I wish would take him*
Mi brother thei he were! *though*

625 "Ac," sche seyd, "bi Him that ous wrought, *But; created*
Al thi precheing helpeth nought, *preaching*
No stond thou never so long. *(No matter how long you) resist*
Bot yif thou wilt graunt me mi thought, *Unless*
Mi love schal be ful dere abought *dearly paid for*
630 With pines hard and strong; *pains*
Mi kerchef and mi clothes anon
Y schal torende doun ichon *tear; every one*
And say with michel wrong, *great*
With strengthe thou hast me todrawe; *violated*
635 Ytake thou schalt be thurch londes lawe[1]
And dempt heighe to hong!" *condemned high to hang*

---

[1] *You shall be arrested according to the laws of the land*

	Than stode that hendy knight ful stille,	
	And in his hert him liked ille,	*he was displeased*
	No word no spac he tho;	*spoke; then*
640	He thought, "Bot y graunt hir wille,	*Unless*
	With hir speche sche wil me spille,	*destroy*
	Er than y passe hir fro;	*Before; from*
	And yif y do mi lord this wrong,	
	With wilde hors and with strong	
645	Y schal be drawe also."	*drawn*
	Loth him was that dede to don,	*Reluctant*
	And wele lother his liif forgon;	*more reluctant; life give up*
	Was him never so wo.	*He was never so woeful*

	And than he thought, withouten lesing,	*lies*
650	Better were to graunt hir asking	
	Than his liif for to spille.	*life; lose*
	Than seyd he to that maiden ying,	*young*
	"For Godes love, heven king,	
	Understond to mi skille.	*Listen to my excuse*
655	Astow art maiden gode and trewe	*As you*
	Bithenk hou oft rape wil rewe	*Think; haste will be regretted*
	And turn to grame wel grille,	*harm; fearful*
	And abide we al this sevennight,	*wait; week*
	As icham trewe gentil knight,	*I am; noble*
660	Y schal graunt the thi wille."	

	Than answerd that bird bright	
	And swore, "Bi Jhesu, ful of might,	
	Thou scapest nought so oway.	*escape not; away*
	Thi treuthe anon thou schalt me plight,	*fidelity; pledge*
665	Astow art trewe gentil knight,	*As you; noble*
	Thou schalt hold that day."	*keep to that day*
	He graunted hir hir wil tho,	*then*
	And plight hem trewthes bothe to,	*pledged fidelity between the two of them*
	And seththen kist tho tuai.	*then; those two*
670	Into hir chaumber sche went ogain,	*chamber; again*
	Than was sche so glad and fain,	*joyful*
	Hir joie sche couthe no man sai.	*could; tell*

	Sir Amis than withouten duelling,	*delay*
	For to kepe his lordes coming,	*prepare for*
675	Into halle he went anon.	*at once*
	When thai were comen fram dere hunting	
	And with him mani an heighe lording	*high lord*
	Into that worthly won,	*stately dwelling*
	After his douhter he asked swithe;	*quickly*
680	Men seyd that sche was glad and blithe,	*joyful*

Hir care was al agon.   *gone*
To eten in halle thai brought that may,   *eat; maiden*
Ful blithe and glad thai were that day
And thonked God ichon.   *everyone*

685   When the lordinges, withouten les,   *lords; lies*
Hendelich were brought on des   *Courteously; high table*
With levedis bright and swete,   *ladies beautiful*
As princes that were proude in pres,   *bold in battle*
Ful richeliche served he wes   *they were*
690   With menske and mirthe to mete.   *dignity; at dinner*
When that maiden that y of told,
Among the birdes that were bold,   *women; joyous*
Ther sche sat in her sete,
On Sir Amis, that gentil knight,   *noble*
695   An hundred time sche cast hir sight,
For no thing wald sche lete.   *leave off (stop)*

On Sir Amis, that knight hendy,
Ever more sche cast hir eyghe,   *eyes*
For no thing wold sche spare.   *let up (stop)*
700   The steward ful of felonie,   *wickedness*
Wel fast he gan hem aspie,   *attentively; watch*
Til he wist of her fare,   *knew; condition*
And bi her sight he parceived tho   *perceived then*
That gret love was bituix hem to,   *between those two*
705   And was agreved ful sare,   *aggrieved; sorely*
And thought he schuld in a while
Bothe with tresoun and with gile   *guile*
Bring hem into care.   *sorrow*

Thus, ywis, that miri may   *sweet maiden*
710   Ete in halle with gamen and play   *Ate; pleasure*
Wele four days other five,   *or*
That ever when sche Sir Amis say,   *saw*
Al hir care was went oway,   *away*
Wele was hir o live.   *alive*
715   Wher that he sat or stode,   *Whether*
Sche biheld opon that frely fode,   *noble young man*
No stint sche for no strive;   *stinted; danger*
And the steward for wrethe sake   *wrath's*
Brought hem bothe in ten and wrake.   *injury; trouble*
720   Wel ivel mot he thrive.   *evilly might*

That riche douke opon a day
On dere hunting went him to play,
And with him wel mani a man;

And Belisaunt, that miri may,   *sweet maiden*
725   To chaumber ther Sir Amis lay,   *where*
       Sche went, as sche wele kan;
       And the steward, withouten les,   *lies*
       In a chaumber bisiden he wes   *nearby*
       And seighe the maiden than   *saw; then*
730   Into chaumber hou sche gan glide;
       For to aspie hem bothe that tide,   *spy on them; time*
       After swithe he ran.   *quickly*

           When that may com into that won,   *maiden; dwelling*
       Sche fond Sir Amis ther alon,   *found*
735   "Hail," sche seyd, that levedi bright,   *lady beautiful*
       "Sir Amis," sche sayd anon,
       "This day a sevennight it is gon,   *week; has passed*
       That trewthe we ous plight.   *fidelity; pledged*
       Therfore icham comen to the,   *I am*
740   To wite, astow art hende and fre   *know, as you are*
       And holden a gentil knight,   *considered*
       Whether wiltow me forsake   *If you will*
       Or thou wilt trewely to me take
       And hold as thou bihight?"   *promised*

745   "Madame," seyd the knight ogain,   *in response*
       "Y wold the spouse now ful fain   *espouse; gladly*
       And hold the to mi wive;
       Ac yif thi fader herd it sain   *But if; said*
       That ich hadde his douhter forlain,   *fornicated with*
750   Of lond he wald me drive.   *Out of the country; would*
       Ac yif ich were king of this lond   *But*
       And hadde more gode in min hond   *possessions*
       Than other kinges five,
       Wel fain y wald spouse the than;   *gladly*
755   Ac, certes, icham a pover man,   *But certainly I am a poor man*
       Wel wo is me o live!"   *alive*

           "Sir knight," seyd that maiden kinde,   *noble*
       "For love of Seyn Tomas of Ynde,
       Whi seystow ever nay?   *say you*
760   No be thou never so pover of kinde,   *Regardless of how poor of kin*
       Riches anough y may the finde
       Bothe bi night and day."
       That hende knight bithought him than   *thought to himself*
       And in his armes he hir nam   *took*
765   And kist that miri may;   *sweet maiden*
       And so thai plaid in word and dede,   *played*

That he wan hir maidenhede,   *won; maidenhead*
Er that sche went oway.   *Before; away*

   And ever that steward gan abide   *remained*
770 Alon under that chaumber side,
Their consail hem for to here.   *secrets*
In at an hole, was nought to wide,
He seighe hem bothe in that tide   *saw; time*
Hou thai seten yfere.   *sat together*
775 And when he seyghe hem bothe with sight,   *saw*
Sir Amis and that bird bright,   *woman lovely*
The doukes douhter dere,
Ful wroth he was and egre of mode,   *angry; fierce of manner*
And went oway, as he were wode,   *away; mad*
780 Her conseil to unskere.   *Their secret; disclose*

   When the douke come in to that won   *dwelling*
The steward ogain him gan gon,   *up to him went*
Her conseyl forto unwrain,   *Their secret; reveal*
"Mi lord, the douke," he seyd anon,
785 "Of thine harm, bi Seyn Jon,
Ichil the warn ful fain;   *I will; gladly*
In thi court thou hast a thef,   *thief*
That hath don min hert gref,   *heart grief*
Schame it is to sain,   *Shame; say*
790 For, certes, he is a traitour strong,
When he with tresoun and with wrong
Thi douhter hath forlain!"   *lain with*

   The riche douke gan sore agrame: *became grievously angry*
"Who hath," he seyd, "don me that schame?
795 Tel me, y the pray!"
"Sir," seyd the steward, "bi Seyn Jame,
Ful wele y can the tel his name,
Thou do him hong this day;   *hang*
It is thi boteler, Sir Amis,   *dispenser*
800 Ever he hath ben traitour, ywis
He hath forlain that may.   *lain with; maiden*
Y seighe it me self, for sothe,   *saw; truly*
And wil aprove biforn hem bothe,   *swear before them*
That thai can nought say nay!"

805   Than was the douke egre of mode,   *fierce of disposition*
He ran to halle, as he were wode,   *mad*
For no thing he nold abide.   *would not stop*
With a fauchoun scharp and gode   *long curved sword*
He smot to Sir Amis ther he stode,   *smote; where*

810	And failed of him biside.	*missed*
	Into a chaumber Sir Amis ran tho	*then*
	And schet the dore bituen hem to	*shut*
	For drede his heved to hide.	*dread; head*
	The douke strok after swiche a dent	*struck; such a blow*
815	That thurch the dore that fauchon went,	*through; long curved sword*
	So egre he was that tide.	*fierce; at that time*
	Al that ever about him stode,	*stood*
	Bisought the douke to slake his mode,	*calm his manner*
	Bothe erl, baroun, and swain;	*young men*
820	And he swore bi Him that dyed on Rode	*died on the Cross*
	He nold for al this worldes gode	*possessions*
	Bot that traitour were slain.	*But*
	"Ich have him don gret honour,	
	And he hath as a vile traitour	
825	Mi douhter forlain;	*lain with*
	Y nold for al this worldes won	*possessions*
	Bot y might the traitour slon	*Unless; slay*
	With min hondes tuain."	*two*
	"Sir," seyd Sir Amis anon,	
830	"Lete thi wrethe first overgon,	*Let your anger; die down*
	Y pray the, par charité!	*for charity*
	And yif thou may prove, bi Sein Jon,	*if*
	That ichave swiche a dede don,	*I have such; done*
	Do me to hong on tre!	*tree*
835	Ac yif ani with gret wrong	*But*
	Hath lowe on ous that lesing strong,	*lied about; lying*
	What bern that he be,	*man*
	He leighth on ous, withouten fail,	*lies about us*
	Ichil aprove it in bataile,	*I will prove it in battle*
840	To make ous quite and fre."	*exonerated and free*
	"Ya," seyd the douke, "wiltow so,	*will you*
	Darstow into bataile go,	*Dare you; battle*
	Al quite and skere you make?"	*To make you all exonerated and cleared*
	"Ya, certes, sir!" he seyd tho,	*then*
845	"And here mi glove y give ther to,	
	He leighe on ous with wrake."	*lies; malice*
	The steward stirt to him than	*started; then*
	And seyd, "Traitour, fals man,	
	Ataint thou schalt be take;	*Convicted*
850	Y seighe it me self this ich day,	*saw; very*
	Where that sche in thi chaumber lay,	
	Your noither it may forsake!"	*Neither of you; deny*

	Thus the steward ever gan say,	*repeatedly said*
	And ever Sir Amis seyd, "Nay,	
855	Ywis, it nas nought so!"	*Indeed; was not*
	Than dede the douke com forth that may,	*called forth that maiden*
	And the steward withstode al way	*persisted*
	And vouwed the dede tho.	*swore*
	The maiden wepe, hir hondes wrong,	*wept; hands wrung*
860	And ever swore hir moder among,	*mother*
	"Certain, it was nought so!"	
	Than seyd the douke, "Withouten fail,	
	It schal be proved in batail	*battle*
	And sen bituen hem to."	*witnessed*

865	Than was atuix hem take the fight	*between; arranged*
	And sett the day a fourtennight,	*at fortnight (two weeks)*
	That mani man schuld it sen.	*should; see*
	The steward was michel of might;	*great*
	In al the court was ther no wight	*person*
870	Sir Amis borwe durst ben.	*Sir Amis' second (guarantor) dared no one be*
	Bot for the steward was so strong,	*Because*
	Borwes anowe he fond among,	*Seconds (guarantors) enough; found*
	Tuenti al bidene.	*Twenty altogether*
	Than seyd thai all with resoun,	*logically*
875	Sir Amis schuld ben in prisoun,	*should be*
	For he no schuld nowhar flen.	*should nowhere flee*

	Than answerd that maiden bright	*answered; beautiful*
	And swore bi Jhesu, ful of might,	
	That were michel wrong,	*great*
880	"Taketh mi bodi for that knight,	
	Til that his day com of fight,	
	And put me in prisoun strong.	
	Yif that the knight wil flen oway	*flee away*
	And dar nought holden up his day,	*dare*
885	Bataile of him to fong,	*Battle; undertake*
	Do me than londes lawe	*according to law*
	For his love to be todrawe	*torn to pieces*
	And heighe on galwes hong."	*high; gallows*

	Hir moder seyd with wordes bold	*said*
890	That with gode wil als sche wold	*good will also she would*
	Ben his borwe also,	*Be; second (guarantor)*
	His day of bataile up to hold,	*battle to guarantee*
	That he as gode knight schold	*should*
	Fight ogain his fo.	*against; foe*
895	Thus tho levedis fair and bright	*those ladies; beautiful*
	Boden for that gentil knight	*Pledged*

	To lain her bodis to.	*To offer their bodies two (both)*
	Than seyd the lordinges everichon,	*lords every one*
	That other borwes wold thai non,	*guarantors needed they none*
900	Bot graunt it schuld be so.	*But allowed*

	When thai had don, as y you say,	
	And borwes founde withouten delay,	
	And graunted al that ther ware,	
	Sir Amis sorwed night and day,	*sorrowed*
905	Al his joie was went oway,	*away*
	And comen was al his care,	
	For that the steward was so strong	
	And hadde the right and he the wrong	*And was in the right*
	Of that he opon him bare.	*bore*
910	Of his liif yaf he nought,	*life gave (cared)*
	Bot of the maiden so michel he thought,	*But; much*
	Might noman morn mare.	*no man mourn more*

	For he thought that he most nede,	*he must*
	Ar that he to bataile yede,	*Before; went*
915	Swere on oth biforn,	*oath before*
	That al so God schuld him spede	*assist*
	As he was giltles of that dede,	
	That ther was on him born;	
	And than thought he, withouten wrong,	
920	He hadde lever to ben anhong	*rather; hanged*
	Than to be forsworn.	
	Ac oft he bisought Jhesu tho,	*But*
	He schuld save hem bothe to,	*both of them*
	That thai ner nought forlorn.	*So that they would not be lost*

925	So if bifel opon a day	
	He mett the levedi and that may	*maiden*
	Under an orchard side.	
	"Sir Amis," the levedy gan say,	*lady*
	"Whi mornestow so withouten play?	*Why mourn you*
930	Tel me that sothe this tide.	
	No drede the nought," sche seyd than,	*dread you*
	"For to fight with thi foman,	*enemy*
	Whether thou wilt go or ride,	*walk or ride*
	So richeliche y schal the schrede,	*richly; you equip*
935	Tharf the never have of him drede,	*Need you*
	Thi bataile to abide."	*battle; sustain*

	"Madame," seyd that gentil knight,	
	"For Jhesus love, ful of might,	
	Be nought wroth for this dede.	

940	Ich have that wrong and he the right,	*I*
	Therfore icham aferd to fight,	*I am afraid*
	Al so God me spede,	*As God gives me fortune*
	For y mot swere, withouten faile,	*must*
	Al so God me spede in bataile,	
945	His speche is falshede;	*falsehood*
	And yif y swere, icham forsworn,	*I am*
	Than liif and soule icham forlorn;	*life and soul I am*
	Certes, y can no rede!"	*Certainly; remedy*

Than seyd that levedi in a while,
950 "No mai ther go non other gile   *Is there no other guile*
To bring that traitor doun?"
"Yis, dame," he seyd, "bi Seyn Gile!
Her woneth hennes mani a mile   *There lives hence*
Mi brother, Sir Amiloun,
955 And yif y dorst to gon,   *if I should dare*
Y dorst wele swere bi Seyn Jon,   *dare; swear*
So trewe is that baroun,   *loyal*
His owhen liif to lese to mede,   *His own life to lose as a result*
He wold help me at this nede,
960 To fight with that feloun."   *felon (criminal)*

"Sir Amis," the levedi gan to say,
"Take leve to morwe at day   *tomorrow morning*
And wende in thi jurné.   *travel; journey*
Y schal say thou schalt in thi way
965 Hom in to thine owhen cuntray,   *own country*
Thi fader, thi moder to se;
And when thou comes to thi brother right,
Pray him, as he is hendi knight
And of gret bounté,   *generosity*
970 That he the batail for ous fong   *battle; undertake*
Ogain the steward that with wrong   *Against*
Wil stroie ous alle thre."   *destroy*

A morwe Sir Amis made him yare   *In the morning; ready*
And toke his leve for to fare   *leave; travel*
975 And went in his jurnay.   *journey*
For nothing nold he spare,   *refrain from*
He priked the stede that him bare   *spurred; horse; bore*
Bothe night and day.
So long he priked withouten abod   *delay*
980 The stede that he on rode
In a fer cuntray   *far country*
Was overcomen and fel doun ded;   *exhausted*

Tho couthe he no better red,   *Then he knew no better plan*
His song was, "Waileway!"   *wellaway*

985 And when it was bifallen so,
   Nedes afot he most go,   *By need he must go on foot*
   Ful careful was that knight.   *unhappy*
   He stiked up his lappes tho,   *took; hems then*
   In his way he gan to go,
990 To hold that he bihight;   *To keep to what he intended*
   And al that day so long he ran,
   In to a wilde forest he cam
   Bituen the day and the night.
   So strong slepe yede him on,   *came*
995 To win al this warldes won,   *world's possessions*
   No ferther he no might.

   The knight, that was so hende and fre,
   Wel fair he layd him under a tre   *tree*
   And fel in slepe that tide.   *time*
1000 Al that night stille lay he,
   Til amorwe men might yse   *in the morning; see*
   The day bi ich a side.   *on all sides*
   Than was his brother, Sir Amiloun,
   Holden a lord of gret renoun   *Considered*
1005 Over al that cuntré wide,   *country*
   And woned fro thennes that he lay *lived from where he lay*
   Bot half a jorné of a day,   *But; journey*
   Noither to go no ride.   *Whether walking or riding*

   As Sir Amiloun, that hendi knight,
1010 In his slepe he lay that night,
   In sweven he mett anon   *dream; dreamed*
   That he seighe Sir Amis bi sight,   *saw*
   His brother, that was trewethe plight, *pledged to loyalty*
   Bilapped among his fon; *Surrounded by his enemies*
1015 Thurch a bere wilde and wode *By a bear wild and mad*
   And other bestes, that bi him stode,   *stood*
   Bisett he was to slon; *He was about to be killed*
   And he alon among hem stode
   As a man that couthe no gode;   *expected*
1020 Wel wo was him bigon.

   When Sir Amiloun was awake,
   Gret sorwe he gan for him make
   And told his wiif ful yare   *wife immediately*
   Hou him thought he seighe bestes blake *saw beasts black*
1025 About his brother with wrake   *vengefulness*

To sle with sorwe and care.   *slay*
"Certes," he seyd, "with sum wrong   *Certainly*
He is in peril gret and strong,
Of blis he is ful bare."   *barren*
1030   And than seyd he, "For sothe ywis,
Y no schal never have joie no blis,
Til y wite hou he fare."   *know; fares*

As swithe he stirt up in that tide,   *Immediately; started*
Ther nold he no leng abide,
1035   Bot dight him forth anon,   *But prepared*
And al his meine bi ich a side   *company on each side*
Busked hem redi to ride,   *Prepared*
With her lord for to gon;   *their*
And he bad al that ther wes,   *bade all who were there*
1040   For Godes love held hem stille in pes,   *hold themselves*
He bad hem so ich-chon,   *every one*
And swore bi Him that schop mankende,   *made mankind*
Ther schuld no man with him wende,   *go*
Bot himself alon.

1045   Ful richeliche he gan him schrede   *richly; dress*
And lepe astite opon his stede,   *immediately*
For nothing he nold abide.   *would not wait*
Al his folk he gan forbede   *forbade (excluded)*
That non so hardi were of dede,   *none so hardy was in deeds*
1050   After him noither go no ride.   *After him neither to walk nor ride*
So al that night he rode til day,
Til he com ther Sir Amis lay   *where*
Up in that forest wide.
Than seighe he a weri knight forgon   *saw; weary; exhausted*
1055   Under a tre slepeand alon;   *sleeping*
To him he went that tide.

He cleped to him anon right,   *said*
"Arise up, felawe, it is light
And time for to go!"
1060   Sir Amis biheld up with his sight
And knewe anon that gentil knight,
And he knewe him also.
That hendi knight, Sir Amiloun,
Of his stede light adoun,   *Got down off his horse*
1065   And kist hem bothe to.   *kissed; two*
"Brother," he seyd, "whi listow here   *lie you down*
With thus mornand chere?   *such mournful disposition*
Who hath wrought the this wo?"

"Brother," seyd Sir Amis tho,
1070 "Ywis, me nas never so wo
Seththen that y was born;   *Since*
For seththen that thou was went me fro,
With joie and michel blis also
Y served mi lord biforn.
1075 Ac the steward ful of envie,
With gile and with trecherie,   *guile; treachery*
He hath me wrought swiche sorn;   *such sorrow*
Bot thou help me at this nede,   *Unless*
Certes, y can no nother rede,   *know no other remedy (course of action)*
1080 Mi liif, it is forlorn!"

"Brother," Seyd Sir Amiloun,
"Whi hath the steward, that feloun,   *criminal (felon)*
Ydon the al this schame?"   *Done; shame*
"Certes," he seyd, "with gret tresoun
1085 He wald me driven al adoun   *would*
And hath me brought in blame."
Than told Sir Amis al that cas,
Hou he and that maiden was
Bothe togider ysame,   *in each other's company*
1090 And hou the steward gan hem wrain,   *accuse*
And hou the douke wald him have slain   *would*
With wrethe and michel grame.   *wrath; anger*

And also he seyd, yplight,   *truly*
Hou he had boden on him fight,   *offered*
1095 Batail of him to fong,   *Battle; undertake*
And hou in court was ther no wight,   *person*
To save tho tuay levedis bright,   *To save those two beautiful ladies*
Durst ben his borwe among,   *Dared; second*
And hou he most, withouten faile,
1100 Swere, ar he went to bataile,   *before; battle*
It war a lesing ful strong;   *falsehood*
"And forsworn man schal never spede;   *succeed*
Certes, therfore y can no rede,   *know no relief*
'Allas' may be mi song!"

1105   When that Sir Amis had al told,
Hou that the fals steward wold
Bring him doun with mode,   *passion*
Sir Amiloun with wordes bold
Swore, "Bi Him that Judas sold   *i.e., betrayed*
1110 And died opon the Rode,   *Cross*
Of his hope he schal now faile,
And y schal for the take bataile,   *battle*

Thei that he wer wode;   *Even if he is mad*
Yif y may mete him aright,
1115 With mi brond, that is so bright,   *sword*
Y schal sen his hert blode!   *see his heart's blood*

Ac brother," he seyd, "have al mi wede,   *clothes*
And in thi robe y schal me schrede,   *dress*
Right as the self it ware;
1120 And y schal swere so God me spede
As icham giltles of that dede,   *I am*
That he opon the bare."   *brought*
Anon tho hendi knightes to   *those; two*
Alle her wede chaunged tho,   *clothes; then*
1125 And when thai were al yare,   *ready*
Than seyd Sir Amiloun, "Bi Seyn Gile,
Thus man schal the schrewe bigile,   *villain; beguile*
That wald the forfare!   *would you destroy*

Brother," he seyd, "wende hom now right
1130 To mi levedi, that is so bright,   *lady; beautiful*
And do as y schal the sain;   *tell (say)*
And as thou art a gentil knight,
Thou ly bi hir in bed ich night,   *each*
Til that y com ogain,   *Until*
1135 And sai thou hast sent thi stede ywis   *horse*
To thi brother, Sir Amis;
Than wil thai be ful fain,   *glad*
Thai wil wene that ich it be;   *think*
Ther is non that schal knowe the,
1140 So liche we be bothe tuain!"   *alike*

And when he hadde thus sayd, yplight,   *truly*
Sir Amiloun, that gentil knight,
Went in his jurnay,
And Sir Amis went hom anon right   *at once*
1145 To his brother levedi so bright,   *brother's lady*
Withouten more delay,
And seyd hou he hadde sent his stede   *horse*
To his brother to riche mede   *as a valuable gift*
Bi a knight of that cuntray;   *By*
1150 And al thai wende of Sir Amis   *thought*
It had ben her lord, ywis,
So liche were tho tuay.

When that Sir Amis hadde ful yare   *had completely*
Told him al of his care,
1155 Ful wele he wend tho,

Litel and michel, lasse and mare,   *Little and much, less and more*
Al that ever in court ware,
Thai thought it hadde ben so.
And when it was comen to the night,
1160 Sir Amis and that levedi bright,
To bed thai gun go;
And whan thai were togider ylayd,
Sir Amis his swerd out braid   *drew*
And layd bituix hem tuo.   *between*

1165   The levedi loked opon him tho
Wrothlich with her eighen tuo,   *Angrily; eyes*
Sche wend hir lord were wode.   *thought; mad*
"Sir," sche seyd, "whi farstow so?   *why do you behave so*
Thus were thou noght won to do,   *used to do*
1170 Who hath changed thi mode?"   *manner*
"Dame," he seyd, "sikerly,   *certainly*
Ich have swiche a malady
That mengeth al mi blod,   *troubles; blood*
And al min bones be so sare,   *sore*
1175 Y nold nought toche thi bodi bare   *I do not want to touch you naked*
For al this warldes gode!"   *world's possessions*

Thus, ywis, that hendy knight
Was holden in that fourtennight   *held; fortnight*
As lord and prince in pride;
1180 Ac he forgat him never a night,
Bituix him and that levedi bright
His swerd he layd biside.
The levedi thought in hir resoun,
It hadde ben hir lord, Sir Amiloun,
1185 That hadde ben sike that tide;
Therfore sche held hir stille tho
And wold speke wordes no mo,
Bot thought his wille to abide.

Now, hende, herkneth, and y schal say
1190 Hou that Sir Amiloun went his way;
For nothing wold he spare.
He priked his stede night and day,   *spurred*
As a gentil knight, stout and gay,
To court he com ful yare   *quickly*
1195 That selve day, withouten fail,   *same*
That was ysett of batail,   *set for battle*
And Sir Amis was nought thare.
Than were tho levedis taken bi hond,

Her juggement to understond,   *judgment to undergo*
1200 With sorwe and sikeing sare.   *sighing sore*

The steward hoved opon a stede   *waited*
With scheld and spere, bataile to bede,   *offer*
Gret bost he gan to blawe;   *proclaim*
Bifor the douke anon he yede   *went*
1205 And seyd, "Sir, so God the spede,
Herken to mi sawe!   *speech*
This traitour is out of lond ywent;
Yif he were here in present,
He schuld ben hong and drawe;
1210 Therefore ich aske jugement,
That his borwes be tobrent,   *seconds be burned*
As it is londes lawe."

That riche douke, with wrethe and wrake,   *wrath; anger*
He bad men schuld tho levedis take   *those ladies*
1215 And lede hem forth biside;
A strong fer ther was don make   *fire*
And a tonne for her sake,   *barrel*
To bren hem in that tide.   *burn them*
Than thai loked in to the feld   *field*
1220 And seighe a knight with spere and scheld   *saw*
Com prikeand ther with pride.   *spurring*
Than seyd thai everichon, ywis,
"Yonder cometh prikeand Sir Amis!"   *galloping*
And bad thai schuld abide.   *bade; wait*

1225 Sir Amiloun gan stint at no ston,   *rest; milestone*
He priked among hem everichon,   *rode*
To that douke he gan wende.
"Mi lord the douke," he seyd anon,
"For schame lete tho levedis gon,
1230 That er bothe gode and hende,   *are*
For ich am comen hider today   *hither*
For to saven hem, yive y may,   *if*
And bring hem out of bende,   *bonds*
For, certes, it were michel unright
1235 To make roste of levedis bright;   *roast*
Ywis, ye eren unkende."   *would be unnatural*

Than ware tho levedis glad and blithe,
Her joie couthe thai noman kithe,   *Their; could; no man tell*
Her care was al oway;
1240 And seththen, as ye may list and lithe,   *then; listen and hear*
Into the chaunber thai went aswithe,   *quickly*

Withouten more delay,
And richeliche thai schred that knight   *dressed*
With helme and plate and brini bright,   *helmet; armor; coat of mail*
1245 His tire, it was ful gay.   *attire*
And when he was opon his stede,
That God hem schuld save and spede   *support*
Mani man bad that day.   *prayed*

As he com prikand out of toun,   *galloping*
1250 Com a voice fram heven adoun,
That noman herd bot he,
And sayd, "Thou knight, Sir Amiloun,
God, that suffred passioun,
Sent the bode bi me;   *warning*
1255 Yif thou this bataile underfong,   *undertake*
Thou schalt have an eventour strong   *adventure*
Within this yeres thre;
And or this thre yere be al gon,   *before*
Fouler mesel nas never non   *leper*
1260 In the world, than thou schal be!

"Ac for thou art so hende and fre,
Jhesu sent the bode bi me,   *warning*
To warn the anon;
So foule a wreche thou schalt be,
1265 With sorwe and care and poverté
Nas never non wers bigon.   *worse*
Over al this world, fer and hende,   *far and near*
Tho that be thine best frende   *Those*
Schal be thi most fon,   *greatest enemies*
1270 And thi wiif and alle thi kinne   *kin*
Schul fle the stede thatow art inne,   *place that you*
And forsake the ichon."   *every one*

That knight gan hove stille so ston   *stand; stone*
And herd tho wordes everichon,
1275 That were so gret and grille.   *fearsome*
He nist what him was best to don,   *did not know*
To flen, other to fighting gon;   *flee, or*
In hert him liked ille.
He thought, "Yif y beknowe mi name,   *make known*
1280 Than schal mi brother go to schame,
With sorwe thai schul him spille.   *kill*
Certes," he seyd, "for drede of care
To hold mi treuthe schal y nought spare,
Lete God don alle His wille."

1285	Al the folk ther was, ywis,	
	Thai wend it had ben Sir Amis	*believed*
	That bataile schuld bede;	*offer*
	He and the steward of pris	*excellence*
	Were brought bifor the justise	
1290	To swere for that dede.	
	The steward swore the pople among,	*people*
	As wis as he seyd no wrong,	*Surely*
	God help him at his nede;	
	And Sir Amiloun swore and gan to say	
1295	As wis as he never kist that may,	*Surely; maiden*
	Our Levedi schuld hem spede.	*reward*

When thai hadde sworn, as y you told,
To biker tho bernes were ful bold *fight*
And busked hem for to ride. *prepared*
1300 Al that ther was, yong and old,
Bisought God yif that He wold
Help Sir Amis that tide.
On stedes that were stithe and strong *brave*
Thai riden togider with schaftes long, *spear-shafts*
1305 Til thai toschiverd bi ich a side; *broke into pieces*
And than drough thai swerdes gode *drew*
And hewe togider, as thai were wode, *struck (with weapons); mad*
For nothing thai nold abide. *would not stop*

Tho gomes, that were egre of sight, *men; fierce*
1310 With fauchouns felle thai gun to fight *long curved swords deadly*
And ferd as thai were wode. *proceeded as if*
So hard thai hewe on helmes bright *struck (with weapons); helmets*
With strong strokes of michel might, *great*
That fer biforn out stode; *That fire (sparks) flashed out*
1315 So hard thai hewe on helme and side, *struck; helmet; side (of his body)*
Thurch dent of grimly woundes wide, *stroke; severe*
That thai sprad al of blod. *were covered*
Fram morwe to none, withouten faile, *morning to noon*
Bituixen hem last the bataile,
1320 So egre thai were of mode. *fierce; mood*

Sir Amiloun, as fer of flint, *sparks from a flint*
With wrethe anon to him he wint *wrath; went*
And smot a stroke with main; *force*
Ac he failed of his dint, *Although; blow*
1325 The stede in the heved he hint *head; hit*
And smot out al his brain. *smote*
The stede fel ded doun to grounde;
Tho was the steward that stounde *Then; moment*

Ful ferd he schuld be slain.   *afraid*
1330 Sir Amiloun light adoun of his stede,   *i.e., dismounted*
To the steward afot he yede   *went*
And halp him up ogain.   *helped*

"Arise up, steward," he seyd anon,
"To fight thou schalt afot gon,
1335 For thou hast lorn thi stede;   *lost*
For it were gret vilani, bi Seyn Jon,
A liggeand man for to slon,   *prostrate; slay*
That were yfallen in nede."
That knight was ful fre to fond   *willing to test (him)*
1340 And tok the steward bi the hond
And seyd, "So God me spede,   *As God give me success*
Now thou schalt afot go,
Y schal fight afot also,
And elles were gret falshed."   *else; treachery*

1345   The steward and that douhti man
Anon togider thai fight gan
With brondes bright and bare;   *swords; drawn*
So hard togider thai fight than,
Til al her armour o blod ran,
1350 For nothing nold thai spare.
The steward smot to him that stounde   *moment*
On his schulder a gret wounde   *shoulder*
With his grimly gare,   *formidable weapon*
That thurch that wounde, as ye may here,
1355 He was knowen with reweli chere,   *sad countenance*
When he was fallen in care.

Than was Sir Amiloun wroth and wode,   *angry and mad*
Whan al his amour ran o blode,
That ere was white so swan;   *white as a swan*
1360 With a fauchoun scharp and gode   *long curved sword*
He smot to him with egre mode   *fierce disposition*
Al so a douhti man,
That even fro the schulder blade
Into the brest the brond gan wade,   *make its way*
1365 Thurchout his hert it ran.
The steward fel adoun ded,   *dead*
Sir Amiloun strok of his hed,   *off*
And God he thonked it than.

Alle the lordinges that ther ware,
1370 Litel and michel, lasse and mare,
Ful glad thai were that tide.

The heved opon a spere thai bare; *head*
To toun thai dight hem ful yare, *took themselves readily*
For nothing thai nold abide; *wait*
1375 Thai com ogaines him out of toun *towards*
With a fair processioun
Semliche bi ich a side. *Splendid on every side*
Anon thai ladde him to the tour *lead*
With joie and ful michel honour,
1380 As prince proude in pride.

In to the palais when thai were gon,
Al that was in that worthli won *worthy dwelling*
Wende Sir Amis it ware. *Thought*
"Sir Amis," seyd the douke anon,
1385 "Bifor this lordinges everichon
Y graunt the ful yare, *readily*
For Belisent, that miri may, *sweet maiden*
Thou hast bought hir ful dere today
With grimli woundes sare; *horrible; sore*
1390 Therfore y graunt the now here
Mi lond and mi douhter dere,
To hald for ever mare." *hold; more*

Ful blithe was that hendi knight *happy*
And thonked him with al his might,
1395 Glad he was and fain; *joyful*
In alle the court was ther no wight
That wist wat his name it hight; *That knew what his name was*
To save tho levedis tuain,
Leches swithe thai han yfounde, *Doctors quickly*
1400 That gun to tasty his wounde *examine*
And made him hole ogain,
Than were thai al glad and blithe
And thonked God a thousand sithe *times*
That the steward was slain.

1405 On a day Sir Amiloun dight him yare *prepared himself quickly*
And seyd that he wold fare
Hom into his cuntray
To telle his frendes, lasse and mare,
And other lordinges that there ware,
1410 Hou he had sped that day.
The douke graunted him that tide *offered*
And bede him knightes and miche pride,
And he answerd, "Nay."
Ther schuld noman with him gon,

1415 Bot as swithe him dight anon   *quickly prepared himself*
      And went forth in his way.

          In his way he went alone,
      Most ther noman with him gon,   *Must*
      Noither knight no swain.
1420 That douhti knight of blod and bon,
      No stint he never at no ston   *He stopped at no milestone*
      Til he com hom ogain;
      And Sir Amis, as y you say,
      Waited his coming everi day
1425 Up in the forest plain;
      And so thai mett togider same,
      And he teld him with joie and game
      Hou he hadde the steward slain,

          And hou he schuld spousy to mede   *espouse as a reward*
1430 That ich maide, worthli in wede,   *same*
      That was so comly corn.   *nobly favored*
      Sir Amiloun light of his stede,   *i.e., dismounted*
      And gan to chaungy her wede,   *exchange their clothes*
      As thai hadde don biforn.
1435 "Brother," he seyd, "wende hom ogain."
      And taught him hou he schuld sain,   *And told him what he should say*
      When he com ther thai worn.
      Than was Sir Amis glad and blithe
      And thanked him a thousand sithe   *times*
1440 The time that he was born.

          And when thai schuld wende ato,
      Sir Amis oft thonked him tho
      His cost and his gode dede.
      "Brother," he seyd, "yif it bitide so   *happen*
1445 That the bitide care other wo,   *encounter*
      And of min help hast nede,
      Savelich com other send thi sond,   *Only; messenger*
      And y schal never lenger withstond,   *delay*
      Al so God me spede;
1450 Be it in peril never so strong,
      Y schal the help in right and wrong,
      Mi liif to lese to mede."   *to lose as a consequence*

          Asonder than thai gun wende;
      Sir Amiloun, that knight so hende,   *gentle (kind)*
1455 Went hom in that tide
      To his levedi that was unkende,   *cruel (unnatural)*
      And was ful welcome to his frende,

As prince proude in pride;
And when it was comen to the night,
1460 Sir Amiloun and that levedi bright
In bedde were layd biside;
In his armes he gan hir kis
And made his joie and michel blis,
For nothing he nold abide.

1465   The levedi astite asked him tho   *immediately*
Whi that he hadde farn so   *behaved*
Al that fourtennight,
Laid his swerd bituen hem to,
That sche no durst nought for wele no wo
1470 Touche his bodi aright.
Sir Amiloun bithought him than
His brother was a trewe man,
That hadde so done, aplight.   *truly*
"Dame," he seyd, "ichil the sain   *I will say to you*
1475 And telle the that sothe ful fain,   *truth full gladly*
Ac wray me to no wight."   *But betray*

The levedi astite him frain gan,   *immediately began to ask him*
For His love, that this warld wan,
Telle hir whi it ware.
1480 Than astite that hendy man,
Al the sothe he teld hir than,
To court hou he gan fare,
And hou he slough the steward strong,
That with tresoun and with wrong
1485 Wold have his brother forfare,   *destroyed*
And hou his brother that hendy knight
Lay with hir in bed ich night
While that he was thare.

The levedi was ful wroth, yplight,   *truly*
1490 And oft missayd hir lord that night   *criticized*
With speche bituix hem to,
And seyd, "With wrong and michel unright
Thou slough ther a gentil knight;   *slew*
Ywis, it was ivel ydo!"   *evilly done*
1495 "Dame," he seyd, "bi heven king,
Y no dede it for non other thing
Bot to save mi brother fro wo,
And ich hope, yif ich hadde nede,
His owhen liif to lesse to mede,   *lessen (shorten) to bring comfort*
1500 He wald help me also."

Al thus, in gest as we sain,   *stories*
Sir Amis was ful glad and fain,   *joyful*
To court he gan to wende;
And when he come to court ogain
1505   With erl, baroun, knight and swain,
Honoured he was, that hende.
That riche douke tok him bi hond
And sesed him in alle his lond,   *gave*
To held withouten ende;
1510   And seththen with joie opon a day
He spoused Belisent, that may,   *maiden*
That was so trewe and kende.   *pleasing*

Miche was that semly folk in sale,   *hall*
That was samned at that bridale   *gathered; wedding*
1515   When he hadde spoused that flour,   *married*
Of erls, barouns, mani and fale,   *many and plenteous*
And other lordinges gret and smale,
And levedis bright in bour.
A real fest thai gan to hold   *royal*
1520   Of erls and of barouns bold
With joie and michel honour;
Over al that lond est and west
Than was Sir Amis helden the best
And chosen for priis in tour.   *excellence*

1525   So within tho yeres to   *two*
A wel fair grace fel hem tho,
As God almighti wold;   *willed*
The riche douke dyed hem fro   *died*
And his levedi dede also,   *wife died*
1530   And graven in grete so cold.   *buried in the ground*
Than was Sir Amis, hende and fre,
Douke and lord of gret pousté   *power*
Over al that lond yhold.
Tuai childer he bigat bi his wive,
1535   The fairest that might bere live,   *bear life*
In gest as it is told.   *story*

Than was that knight of gret renoun
And lord of mani a tour and toun
And douke of gret pousté;   *power*
1540   And his brother, Sir Amiloun,
With sorwe and care was driven adoun,
That ere was hende and fre;   *formerly*
Al so that angel hadde hem told,   *Just as*
Fouler messel that nas non hold   *leper*

1545   In world than was he.
      In gest to rede it is gret rewthe,   *sadness*
      What sorwe he hadde for his treuthe
      Within tho yeres thre.

      And er tho thre yere com to thende   *the end*
1550   He no wist whider he might wende,   *did not know where*
      So wo was him bigon;
      For al that were his best frende,
      And nameliche al his riche kende,   *namely; kin*
      Bicom his most fon;   *enemies*
1555   And his wiif, for sothe to say,
      Wrought him wers bothe night and day   *worse*
      Than thai dede everichon.   *Than any of them did*
      When him was fallen that hard cas,
      A frendeleser man than he was   *more friendless*
1560   Men nist nowhar non.   *Men knew nowhere none*

      So wicked and schrewed was his wiif,   *depraved*
      Sche brac his hert withouten kniif,   *broke; knife*
      With wordes harde and kene,   *sharp*
      And seyd to him, "Thou wreche chaitif,   *wretched coward*
1565   With wrong the steward les his liif,   *lost*
      And that is on the sene;   *obvious*
      Therfore, bi Seyn Denis of Fraunce,
      The is bitid this hard chaunce,   *To you is coming*
      Dathet who the bimene!"   *Cursed be he who laments you*
1570   Wel oft times his honden he wrong,   *hands; wrung*
      As man that thenketh his liif to long,
      That liveth in treye and tene.   *trial and vexation*

      Allas, allas! that gentil knight
      That whilom was so wise and wight,   *once; brave*
1575   That than was wrought so wo,
      Than fram his levedi, fair and bright,
      Out of his owhen chaumber anight
      He was yhote to go,   *called*
      And in his owhen halle o day   *own*
1580   Fram the heighe bord oway   *high table*
      He was ycharged also
      To eten at the tables ende;
      Wald ther no man sit him hende,   *Would; honorably*
      Wel careful was he tho.   *sorrowful*

1585   Bi than that half yere was ago   *By the time*
      That he hadde eten in halle so   *eaten*
      With gode mete and with drink,

His levedi wax ful wroth and wo
And thought he lived to long tho —
1590 Withouten ani lesing —
"In this lond springeth this word,
Y fede a mesel at mi bord,   *leper*
He is so foule a thing,
It is gret spite to al mi kende,   *kin*
1595 He schal no more sitt me so hende,   *near at hand*
Bi Jhesus, heven king!"

On a day sche gan him calle
And seyd, "Sir, it is so bifalle,
For sothe, y telle it te,   *to you*
1600 That thou etest so long in halle,
It is gret spite to ous alle,
Mi kende is wroth with me."   *kin*
The knight gan wepe and seyd ful stille,   *quietly*
"Do me where it is thi wille,   *Put*
1605 Ther noman may me se;   *no man*
Of no more ichil the praye,   *I will you beg*
Bot of a meles mete ich day,
For seynt charité."   *holy charity*

That levedi, for hir lordes sake,
1610 Anon sche dede men timber take,
For nothing wold sche wond,   *hesitate*
And half a mile fram the gate
A litel loge sche lete make,   *lodge; had made*
Biside the way to stond.
1615 And when the loge was al wrought,   *built*
Of his gode no wold he noght,   *possessions*
Bot his gold coupe an hond.   *cup*
When he was in his loge alon,
To God of heven he made his mon   *moan*
1620 And thonked Him of al His sond.   *sending (gifts)*

Into that loge when he was dight   *disposed of*
In al the court was ther no wight   *person*
That wold serve him thare,
To save a gentil child, yplight,   *Except; truly*
1625 Child Owaines his name it hight,   *was called*
For him he wepe ful sare.   *sorely*
That child was trewe and of his kende,   *kin*
His soster sone, he was ful hende;   *sister's; generous*
He sayd to hem ful yare,   *eagerly*
1630 Ywis, he no schuld never wond   *hesitate*

To serven hem fro fot to hond,   *foot to hand*
While he olives ware.   *alive*

    That child, that was so fair and bold,
Owaines was his name ytold,
1635 Wel fair he was of blode.   *blood*
When he was of tuelve yere old,
Amoraunt than was he cald,   *called*
Wel curteys, hend and gode.
Bi his lord ich night he lay   *each*
1640 And feched her livere ever day   *fetched them supplies (of food)*
To her lives fode.   *For; feeding*
When ich man made gle and song,   *glee*
Ever for his lord among
He made dreri mode.   *sad manner*

1645   Thus Amoraunt, as y you say,
Com to court ich day,
No stint he for no strive.   *He stinted no effort*
Al that ther was gan him pray   *Everyone there bade him*
To com fro that lazer oway,   *leper*
1650 Than schuld he the and thrive.   *prosper*
And he answerd with milde mode   *manner*
And swore bi Him that dyed on Rode
And tholed woundes five,   *suffered*
For al this worldes gode to take
1655 His lord nold he never forsake
Whiles he ware olive.

    Bi than the tuelmoneth was al gon,   *year*
Amorant went into that won   *residence*
For his lordes liveray;   *livery*
1660 The levedi was ful wroth anon
And comaunde hir men everichon
To drive that child oway,   *betrayed*
And swore bi Him that Judas sold,
Thei his lord for hunger and cold   *Though*
1665 Dyed ther he lay,
He schuld have noither mete no drink,
No socour of non other thing
For hir after that day.   *From*

    That child wrong his honden tuain
1670 And weping went hom ogain
With sorwe and sikeing sare.   *sighing*
That godeman gan him frain   *question*
And bad him that he schuld him sain   *tell*

	And telle him whi it ware.	*why it was*
1675	And he answerd and seyd tho,	*then*
	"Ywis, no wonder thei me be wo,	
	Mine hert, it breketh for care;	
	Thi wiif hath sworn with gret mode	*force*
	That sche no schal never don ous gode;	*do us good*
1680	Allas, hou schal we fare?"	

	"A, God help!" seyd that gentil knight,	
	"Whilom y was man of might,	*Formerly*
	To dele mete and cloth,	*dispense food and clothing*
	And now icham so foule a wight	*I am; person*
1685	That al that seth on me bi sight,	
	Mi liif is hem ful loth.	*loathsome*
	Sone," he seyd, "lete thi wepeing,	*leave off*
	For this is now a strong tiding,	*harsh news*
	That may we se for soth;	
1690	For, certes, y can non other red,	*I know no other counsel*
	Ous bihoveth to bid our brede,	*It behooves us to beg our bread*
	Now y wot hou it goth."	*[That] I know how it goes*

	Amorwe astite as it was light,	*In the morning as soon as*
	The child and that gentil knight	
1695	Dight hem for to gon,	*Prepared themselves*
	And in her way thai went ful right	
	To begge her brede, as thai hadde tight,	*intended*
	For mete no hadde thai none.	*food; none*
	So long thai went up and doun	
1700	Til thai com to a chepeing toun,	*market town*
	Five mile out of that won,	*area*
	And sore wepeand fro dore to dore,	*weeping*
	And bad here mete for Godes love,	*begged their food*
	Ful ivel couthe thai theron.	*They knew little about that (i.e., begging)*

1705	So in that time, ich understond,	
	Gret plenté was in that lond,	*plenty*
	Bothe of mete and drink;	
	That folk was ful fre to fond	*gracious in action*
	And brought hem anough to hond	
1710	Of al kines thing;	*kinds of*
	For the gode man was so messais tho,	*wretched then*
	And for the child was fair also,	
	Hem loved old and ying,	*Old and young loved them*
	And brought hem anough of al gode;	
1715	Than was the child blithe of mode	*joyful of spirit*
	And lete be his wepeing.	*stopped*

Than wex the gode man fote so sare — *Then the good man became so footsore*
That he no might no forther fare
For al this worldes gode;
1720 To the tounes ende that child him bare
And a loge he bilt him thare, — *lodging*
As folk to chepeing yode; — *Where; market went*
And as that folk of that cuntray
Com to chepeing everi day,
1725 Thai gat hem lives fode; — *food*
And Amoraunt oft to toun gan go
And begged hem mete and drink also,
When hem most nede atstode. — *When they stood at greatest need*

Thus in gest rede we
1730 Thai duelled there yeres thre,
That child and he also,
And lived in care and poverté
Bi the folk of that cuntré,
As thai com to and fro,
1735 So that in the ferth yere — *fourth year*
Corn bigan to wex dere, — *Grain; become scarce*
That hunger bigan to go, — *increase*
That ther was noither eld no ying — *old nor young*
That wald yif hem mete no drink, — *would give*
1740 Wel careful were thai tho. — *Very sad; then*

Amorant oft to toun gan gon,
Ac mete no drink no gat he non,
Noither at man no wive. — *wife (woman)*
When thai were togider alon,
1745 Reweliche thai gan maken her mon, — *Ruefully; lament*
Wo was hem o live;
And his levedi, for sothe to say,
Woned ther in that cuntray — *Lived*
Nought thennes miles five, — *Not five miles thence*
1750 And lived in joie bothe night and day,
Whiles he in sorwe and care lay,
Wel ivel mot sche thrive!

On a day, as thai sete alon, — *sat*
That hendi knight gan meken his mon
1755 And seyd to the child that tide,
"Sone," he seyd, "thou most gon
To mi levedi swithe anon, — *at once*
That woneth here biside, — *dwells; nearby*
Bid hir, for Him that died on Rode,
1760 Sende me so michel of al mi gode,

An asse, on to ride,
And out of lond we wil fare
To begge our mete with sorwe and care,
No lenger we nil abide."   *will not stay*

1765   Amoraunt to court is went
          Bifor that levedi fair and gent,   *well-born*
          Wel hendeliche seyd hir anon,   *courteously*
          "Madame," he seyd, "verrament,   *truly*
          As messanger mi lord me sent,
1770 For himself may nought gon,
          And praieste with milde mode   *begs; mild manner*
          Sende him so michel of al his gode
          As an asse to riden opon,
          And out of lond we schulen yfere,   *will travel*
1775 No schal we never com eft here,   *afterwards*
          Thei hunger ous schuld slon."   *Though; slay*

          The levedi seyd sche wald ful fain   *gladly*
          Sende him gode asses tuain,
          With thi he wald oway go   *Provided that*
1780 So fer that he never eft com ogain.   *far; after; again*
          "Nat, certes, dame," the child gan sain,
          "Thou sest ous never eft mo."   *will see*
          Than was the levedi glad and blithe
          And comaund him an asse as swithe   *at once*
1785 And seyd with wrethe tho,   *anger then*
          "Now ye schul out of lond fare,
          God leve you never to com here mare,   *more*
          And graunt that it be so."

          That child no lenger nold abide,   *would not*
1790 His asse astite he gan bistride   *immediately; bestride*
          And went him hom ogain,
          And told his lord in that tide
          Hou his levedi proude in pride
          Schameliche gan to sain;   *Shamefully*
1795 Opon the asse he sett that knight so hende,
          And out of the cité thai gun wende;   *city*
          Ther of thai were ful fain.
          Thurch mani a cuntré, up an doun,   *Throughout*
          Thai begged her mete fram toun to toun,
1800 Bothe in winde and rain.

          Over al that lond thurch Godes wille
          That hunger wex so gret and grille,   *grew; intense*
          As wide as thai gun go;   *far*

	Almest for hunger thai gan to spille,	*die*
1805	Of brede thai no hadde nought half her fille,	*bread*
	Ful careful were thai tho.	*then*
	Than seyd the knight opon a day,	
	"Ous bihoveth selle our asse oway,	*It behooves us*
	For we no have gode no mo,	*possessions no more*
1810	Save mi riche coupe of gold,	*Except; cup*
	Ac certes, that schal never be sold,	
	Thei hunger schuld me slo."	*Though; slay*

	Than Amoraunt and Sir Amiloun,	
	With sorwe and care and reweful roun	*speech*
1815	Erliche in a morning	*Early*
	Thai went hem to a chepeing toun,	*themselves; market town*
	And when the knight was light adoun,	*dismounted*
	Withouten ani duelling,	*delay*
	Amoraunt went to toun tho,	*then*
1820	His asse he ladde with him also	*led*
	And sold it for five schilling.	
	And while that derth was so strong,	*scarcity*
	Ther with thai bought hem mete among,	*food*
	When thai might gete no thing.	

1825	And when her asse was ysold	
	For five schilling, as y you told,	
	Thai duelled ther dayes thre;	
	Amoraunt wex strong and bold,	
	Of fiftene winter was he old,	
1830	Curtays, hende and fre.	
	For his lord he hadde gret care,	
	And at his rigge he dight him yare	*on his back he placed him readily*
	And bare him out of that cité;	*carried*
	And half a yere and sum del mare	*somewhat more*
1835	About his mete he him bare,	*bore*
	Yblisced mot he be.	*Blessed may*

	Thus Amoraunt, withouten wrong,	
	Bar his lord about so long,	
	As y you tel may.	
1840	That winter com so hard and strong,	
	Oft, "Allas!" it was his song,	
	So depe was that cuntray;	*muddy*
	The way was so depe and slider,	*muddy and slippery*
	Oft times bothe togider	*together*
1845	Thai fel doun in the clay.	
	Ful trewe he was and kinde of blod	

And served his lord with mild mode,   *gentle spirit*
Wald he nought wende oway.

        Thus Amoraunt, as y you say,
1850 Served his lord bothe night and day
        And at his rigge him bare.   *on his back*
        Oft his song was, "Waileway!"
        So depe was that cuntray,
        His bones wex ful sare.   *became; sore*
1855 Al her catel than was spent,   *possessions*
        Save tuelf pans, verrament,   *twelve pence*
        Therwith thai went ful yare
        And bought hem a gode croudewain,   *pushcart*
        His lord he gan ther-in to lain,
1860 He no might him bere namare.   *carry no more*

        Than Amoraunt crud Sir Amiloun   *pushed*
        Thurch mani a cuntré, up and doun,   *many*
        As ye may understond;
        So he com to a cité toun,
1865 Ther Sir Amis, the bold baroun,   *Where*
        Was douke and lord in lond.
        Than seyd the knight in that tide,
        "To the doukes court here biside
        To bring me thider thou fond;   *try*
1870 He is a man of milde mode,   *gentle spirit*
        We schul gete ous ther sum gode
        Thurch grace of Godes sond.   *giving*

        "Ac, leve sone," he seyd than,
        "For His love, that this world wan   *won*
1875 Astow art hende and fre,   *As you*
        Thou be aknowe to no man   *known*
        Whider y schal, no whenes y cam,   *Where I am going or whence I came*
        No what mi name it be."
        He answerd and seyd, "Nay."
1880 To court he went in his way,
        As ye may listen at me,
        And bifor al other pover men   *poor*
        He crud his wain in to the fen;   *pushed; cart; mud*
        Gret diol it was to se.   *sorrow*

1885   So it bifel that selve day,   *same*
        With tong as y you tel may,   *tongue*
        It was midwinter tide,
        That riche douke with gamen and play
        Fram chirche com the right way

1890   As lord and prince with pride.
When he com to the castelgate,   *castle gate*
The pover men that stode therate
Withdrough hem ther beside.   *Withdrew*
With knightes and with serjaunce fale   *men-at-arms many*
1895   He went into that semly sale   *fine hall*
With joie and blis to abide.

In kinges court, as it is lawe,
Trumpes in halle to mete gan blawe,   *Horns in the hall called them to dinner*
To benche went tho bold.
1900   When thai were semly set on rowe,   *appropriately set in place*
Served thai were upon a throwe,   *right away*
As men miriest on mold.   *earth*
That riche douke, withouten les,   *lie*
As a prince served he wes
1905   With riche coupes of gold,   *cups*
And he that brought him to that state
Stode bischet withouten the gate,   *shut out*
Wel sore ofhungred and cold.   *hungered*

Out at the gate com a knight
1910   And a serjaunt wise and wight,   *servant; brave*
To plain hem bothe yfere,   *To amuse themselves together*
And thurch the grace of God Almight   *Almighty*
On Sir Amiloun he cast a sight,   *cast a look*
Hou laith he was of chere.   *hideous; appearance*
1915   And seththen biheld on Amoraunt,   *then looked*
Hou gentil he was and of fair semblaunt,   *appearance*
In gest as ye may here.
Than seyd thai bothe, bi Seyn Jon,
In al the court was ther non
1920   Of fairehed half his pere.   *handsomeness; equal*

The gode man gan to him go,
And hendeliche he asked him tho,   *courteously; then*
As ye may understond,
Fram wat lond that he com fro,
1925   And whi that he stode ther tho,
And whom he served in lond.
"Sir," he seyd, "so God me save,
Icham here mi lordes knave,   *young servant*
That lith in Godes bond;   *lies; service*
1930   And thou art gentil knight of blode,
Bere our erand of sum gode   *Make our errand come to some good*
Thurch grace of Godes sond."   *bounty*

     The gode man asked him anon,
     Yif he wald fro that lazer gon   *leper*
1935 And trewelich to him take;   *faithfully*
     And he seyd he schuld, bi Seyn Jon,
     Serve that riche douke in that won,   *dwelling*
     And richeman he wald him make;
     And he answerd with mild mode   *gentle manner*
1940 And swore bi Him that dyed on Rode
     Whiles he might walk and wake,
     For to winne al this warldes gode,   *world's good*
     His hende lord, that bi him stode,
     Schuld he never forsake.

1945   The gode man wende he hadde ben rage, *believed; mad*
     Or he hadde ben a folesage   *court fool*
     That hadde his witt forlorn,   *wits lost*
     Other he thought that his lord with the foule visage   *Or*
     Hadde ben a man of heighe parage   *parentage*
1950 And of heighe kinde ycorn.   *high kin chosen*
     Therfore he nold no more sain,
     Bot went him in to the halle ogain
     The riche douke biforn,
     "Mi lord," he seyd, "listen to me
1955 The best bourd, bi mi leueté,   *jest; belief*
     Thou herdest seththen thou were born."   *since*

       The riche douke badde him anon   *bade*
     To telle biforn hem everichon
     Withouten more duelling.   *delay*
1960 "Now sir," he seyd, "bi Seyn Jon,
     Ich was out atte gate ygon
     Right now on mi playing;
     Pover men y seighe mani thare,   *Poor; saw*
     Litel and michel, lasse and mare,
1965 Bothe old and ying,
     And a lazer ther y fond;   *leper*
     Herdestow never in no lond   *Heard you*
     Telle of so foule a thing.

       "The lazer lith up in a wain,   *lies; cart*
1970 And is so pover of might and main
     O fot no may he gon;   *On*
     And over him stode a naked swain,   *young man*
     A gentiler child, for sothe to sain,
     In world no wot y non.   *I know none*
1975 He is the fairest gome   *creature*
     That ever Crist yaf Cristendome   *gave*

Or layd liif opon,
And on of the most fole he is									*one; foolish*
That ever thou herdest speke, ywis,
1980 In this worldes won."										*dwelling area*

    Than seyd the riche douke ogain,
"What foly," he seyd, "can he sain?
Is he madde of mode?"										*insane*
"Sir," he seyd, "y bad him fain									*happily*
1985 Forsake the lazer in the wain,									*leper; cart*
That he so over stode,										*took care of*
And in thi servise he schuld be,
Y bihete hem bothe lond and fe,									*offered; land and livestock*
Anough of warldes gode;										*worldly goods*
1990 And he answerd and seyd tho									*then*
He nold never gon him fro;
Therfore ich hold him wode."									*mad*

    Than seyd the douke, "Thei his lord be lorn,					*Though; desolate*
Par aventour, the gode man hath biforn							*Perhaps*
1995 Holpen him at his nede,
Other the child is of his blod yborn,								*Either*
Other he hath him othes sworn									*Or; oaths*
His liif with him to lede.
Whether he be fremd or of his blod,							*a stranger*
2000 The child," he seyd, "is trewe and gode,
Also God me spede.
Yif ichim speke er he wende,									*If I speak to him before*
For that he is so trewe and kende,								*kind (good-natured)*
Y schal quite him his mede!"									*reward him*

2005   That douke astite, as y you told,
Cleped to him a squier bold									*Called*
And hendelich gan hem sain:									*say*
"Take," he sayd, "mi coupe of gold,
As ful of wine astow might hold								*as you*
2010 In thine hondes tuain,
And bere it to the castelgate,
A lazer thou schalt finde therate
Liggeand in a wain.										*Lying in a cart*
Bid him, for the love of Seyn Martin,
2015 He and his page drink this win,								*wine*
And bring me the coupe ogain."

    The squier tho the coupe hent,							*then; took*
And to the castel gat he went,
And ful of win he it bare.

2020   To the lazer he seyd, verrament,
      "This coupe ful of win mi lord the sent,
      Drink it, yife thou dare."   *if*
      The lazer tok forth his coupe of gold,
      Bothe were goten in o mold,   *made; one*
2025   Right as that selve it ware,   *As if they were the same*
      Therin he pourd that win so riche;
      Than were thai bothe ful yliche
      And noither lesse no mare.

      The squier biheld the coupes tho,   *cups then*
2030   First his and his lordes also,
      Whiles he stode hem biforn,
      Ac he no couthe never mo   *could*
      Chese the better of hem to,
      So liche bothe thai worn.   *so alike; were*
2035   Into halle he ran ogain,
      "Certes, sir," he gan to sain,   *say*
      "Mani gode dede thou hast lorn,   *lost*
      And so thou hast lorn this dede now;
      He is a richer man than thou,
2040   Bi the time that God was born."

      The riche douke answerd, "Nay.
      That worth never bi night no day;
      It were ogaines the lawe!"   *against*
      "Yis, sir," he gan to say,
2045   "He is a traitour, bi mi fay,   *by my faith*
      And were wele worth to drawe.   *pull to pieces*
      For when y brought him the win,
      He drough forth a gold coupe fin,   *fine*
      Right as it ware thi nawe;   *your own*
2050   In this world, bi Seyn Jon,
      So wise a man is ther non
      Asundri schuld hem knawe."   *Could tell them apart*

      "Now, certes," seyd Sir Amis tho,   *then*
      "In al this world were coupes nomo   *no more*
2055   So liche in al thing,   *alike*
      Save min and mi brothers also,
      That was sett bituix ous to,
      Token of our parting;
      And yif it be so, with tresoun
2060   Mine hende brother, Sir Amiloun,
      Is slain, withouten lesing.
      And yif he have stollen his coupe oway,

Y schal him sle me self this day,
Bi Jhesu, heven king!"

2065   Fram the bord he resed than   *rose*
        And hent his swerd as a wode man   *seized; madman*
        And drough it out with wrake,   *drew; anger*
        And to the castel gat he ran;   *gate*
        In al the court was ther no man
2070   That him might atake.   *overtake*
        To the lazer he stirt in the wain   *goes; cart*
        And hent him in his honden tuain   *two hands*
        And sleynt him in the lake,   *cast*
        And layd on, as he were wode,   *attacked; mad*
2075   And al that ever about him stode
        Gret diol gan make.   *sorrow*

        "Traitour!" seyd the douke so bold,
        "Where haddestow this coupe of gold   *Whence*
        And hou com thou ther to?
2080   For bi Him that Judas sold,
        Amiloun, mi brother, it hadde in wold,   *possession*
        When that he went me fro!"
        "Ya, certes, sir," he gan to say,
        "It was his in his cuntray,
2085   And now it is fallen so;
        Bot certes, now that icham here,
        The coupe is mine, y bought it dere,
        With right y com ther to."

        Than was the douke ful egre of mod;   *agitated in mind*
2090   Was noman that about him stode
        That durst legge on him hond;   *lay a hand on him*
        He spurned him with his fot
        And laid on, as he were wode,
        With his naked brond,   *bare sword*
2095   And bi the fet the lazer he drough   *feet; leper; dragged*
        And drad on him in the slough;   *terrified him; mudhole*
        For no thing wald he wond,   *hesitate*
        And seyd, "Thef, thou schalt be slawe,   *Thief; slain*
        Bot thou wilt be the sothe aknawe,   *Unless you make known the truth*
2100   Where thou the coupe fond."   *found*

        Child Amoraunt stode the pople among   *people*
        And seye his lord with wough and wrong   *told; evil*
        Hou reweliche he was dight.   *dreadfully; dealt with*
        He was bothe hardi and strong,
2105   The douke in his armes he fong   *seized*

And held him stille upright.
"Sir," he seyd, "thou art unhende   *discourteous*
And of thi werkes unkende,   *ignoble*
To sle that gentil knight.
2110 Wel sore may him rewe that stounde   *time*
That ever for the toke he wounde
To save thi liif in fight.

"And ys thi brother, Sir Amylioun,
That whilom was a noble baroun   *once*
2115 Bothe to ryde and go,
And now with sorwe ys dreve adoun;   *driven*
Nowe God that suffred passioun
Breng him oute of his wo!
For the of blysse he ys bare,   *Because of you he is without happiness*
2120 And thou yeldyst him all with care   *give him grief*
And brekest his bones a two;   *in two*
That he halp the at thi nede,   *helped you*
Well evell aquitest thou his mede,   *pay back his help*
Alas, whi farest thou so?"

2125   When Sir Amis herd him so sain,
He stirt to the knight ogain,   *leaped*
Withouten more delay,
And biclept him in his armes tuain,   *grasped*
And oft, "Allas!" he gan sain;
2130 His song was "Waileway!"
He loked opon his scholder bare
And seighe his grimly wounde thare,   *severe*
As Amoraunt gan him say.
He fel aswon to the grounde   *fainted*
2135 And oft he seyd, "Allas that stounde!"   *time*
That ever he bode that day.   *experienced*

"Allas," he seyd, "mi joie is lorn,   *lost*
Unkender blod nas never born,   *Ignobler blood*
Y not wat y may do;   *don't know*
2140 For he saved mi liif biforn,   *in the past*
Ichave him yolden with wo and sorn   *I have; paid; sorrow*
And wrought him michel wo.
O brother," he seyd, "par charité,
This rewely ded foryif thou me,   *rueful deed forgive*
2145 That ichave smiten the so!"
And he forgave it him also a swithe   *at once*
And kist him wel mani a sithe,
Wepeand with eighen tuo.   *Weeping; eyes*

	Than was Sir Amis glad and fain,	*joyful*
2150	For joie he wepe with his ain	*eyes*
	And hent his brother than,	*seized*
	And tok him in his armes tuain,	*grasped*
	Right til he com into the halle ogain,	
	No bar him no nother man.	
2155	The levedi tho in the halle stode	
	And wend hir lord hadde ben wode,	*thought; mad*
	Ogaines him hye ran.	*Towards; she*
	"Sir," sche seyd, "wat is thi thought?	
	Whi hastow him into halle ybrought	
2160	For Him that this world wan?"	*won*

	"O dame," he seyd, "bi Seyn Jon,	
	Me nas never so wo bigon,	
	Yif thou it wost understond,	*would*
	For better knight in world is non,	
2165	Bot almost now ichave him slon	*slain*
	And schamely driven to schond;	*shamefully; harm*
	For it is mi brother, Sir Amiloun,	
	With sorwe and care is dreven adoun,	
	That er was fre to fond."	*noble in proof*
2170	The levedi fel aswon to grounde	*in a faint*
	And wepe and seyd, "Allas that stounde!"	
	Wel sore wrengand hir hond.	*wringing*

	As foule a lazer as he was,	
	The levedi kist him in that plas,	*place*
2175	For nothing wold sche spare,	
	And oft time sche seyd, "Allas!"	
	That him was fallen so hard a cas,	*fortune*
	To live in sorwe and care.	
	Into hir chaumber she gan him lede	*lead*
2180	And kest of al his pover wede	*cast off; poor clothing*
	And bathed his bodi al bare,	*naked*
	And to a bedde swithe him brought;	*quickly*
	With clothes riche and wele ywrought;	*well made*
	Ful blithe of him thai ware.	

	And thus in gest as we say,	*story*
2185	Tuelmoneth in her chaumber he lay,	*Twelve-month (a year)*
	Ful trewe thai ware and kinde.	
	No wold thai nick him with no nay,	*deny him nothing*
	What so ever he asked night or day,	
2190	It nas never bihinde;	*slow in coming*
	Of everich mete and everi drink	
	Thai had hemselve, withouten lesing,	

Thai were him bothe ful minde.
And bithan the tuelmonth was ago,   *by the time that*
2195   A ful fair grace fel hem tho,   *chance befell*
In gest as we finde.

So it bifel opon a night,
As Sir Amis, that gentil knight,
In slepe thought as he lay,
2200   An angel com fram heven bright
And stode biforn his bed ful right
And to him thus gan say:
Yif he wald rise on Cristes morn,   *Christmas morning*
Swiche time as Jhesu Crist was born,   *Such*
2205   And slen his children tuay,   *kill*
And alien his brother with the blode,   *anoint*
Thurch Godes grace, that is so gode,
His wo schuld wende oway.

Thus him thought al tho thre night
2210   An angel out of heven bright
Warned him ever more
Yif he wald do as he him hight,   *bade*
His brother schuld ben as fair a knight
As ever he was biforn,
2215   Ful blithe was Sir Amis tho,   *happy; then*
Ac for his childer him was ful wo,
For fairer ner non born.
Wel loth him was his childer to slo,   *loath; slay*
And wele lother his brother forgo,   *more loath; abandon*
2220   That is so kinde ycorn.   *highly born*

Sir Amiloun met that night also   *dreamed*
That an angel warned him tho   *then*
And seyd to him ful yare,   *fairly*
Yif his brother wald his childer slo,   *slay*
2225   The hert blod of hem to   *two*
Might bring him out of care.
A morwe Sir Amis was ful hende   *gracious*
And to his brother he gan wende   *turned*
And asked him of his fare;
2230   And he him answerd ogain ful stille,
"Brother, ich abide her Godes wille,   *await here*
For y may do na mare."   *no more*

Al so thai sete togider thare
And speke of aventours, as it ware,   *adventures*
2235   Tho knightes hende and fre,   *Those*

Than seyd Sir Amiloun ful yare,
"Brother, y nil nought spare   *refrain*
To tel the in privité.   *secrecy*
Me thought tonight in me sweven   *dream*
2240   That an angel com fram heven;
For sothe, he told me
That thurch the blod of thin children to   *two*
Y might aschape out of mi wo,   *escape*
Al hayl and hole to be!"   *hail and whole*

2245   Than thought the douk, withouten lesing,
For to slen his childer so ying,   *young*
It were a dedli sinne;   *deadly*
And than thought he, bi heven king,
His brother out of sorwe bring,
2250   For that nold he nought blinne.   *not cease to try*
So it bifel on Cristes night,
Swiche time as Jhesu, ful of might,
Was born to save mankunne,   *mankind*
To chirche to wende al that ther wes,
2255   Thai dighten hem, withouten les,   *prepared themselves*
With joie and worldes winne.   *pleasure*

      Than thai were redi for to fare,   *When*
The douke bad al that ther ware,
To chirche thai schuld wende,
2260   Litel and michel, lasse and mare,
That non bileft in chaumber thare,   *remained*
As thai wald ben his frende,
And seyd he wald himselve that night
Kepe his brother that gentil knight
2265   That was so god and kende.
Than was ther non that durst say nay;
To chirche thai went in her way,
At hom bileft tho hende.

      The douke wel fast gan aspie   *notice*
2270   The kays of the noricerie,   *keys; nursery*
Er than thai schuld gon,   *Before*
And priveliche he cast his eighe   *secretly*
And aparceived ful witterlye   *noticed full well*
Where that thai hadde hem don.   *placed*
2275   And when thai were to chirche went,
Than Sir Amis, verrament,
Was bileft alon.
He tok a candel fair and bright

And to the kays he went ful right   *keys*
2280   And tok hem oway ichon.   *each one*

Alon him self, withouten mo,
Into the chaumber he gan to go,
Ther that his childer were,   *Where*
And biheld hem bothe to,
2285   Hou fair thai lay togider tho   *then*
And slepe bothe yfere.   *together*
Than seyd himselve, "Bi Seyn Jon,
It were gret rewethe you to slon,   *slay*
That God hath bought so dere!"
2290   His kniif he had drawen that tide,
For sorwe he sleynt oway biside   *withdraw*
And wepe with reweful chere.

Than he hadde wopen ther he stode,   *When; wept where*
Anon he turned ogain his mode   *again his mind*
2295   And sayd withouten delay,
"Mi brother was so kinde and gode,
With grimly wounde he schad his blod   *horrible; shed*
For mi love opon a day;
Whi schuld y than mi childer spare,
2300   To bring mi brother out of care?
O, certes," he seyd, "nay!
To help mi brother now at this nede,
God graunt me therto wele to spede,
And Mari, that best may!"   *maiden*

2305   No lenger stint he no stode,   *stopped; moment*
Bot hent his kniif with dreri mode   *grasped; sad countenance*
And tok his children tho;   *took; then*
For he nold nought spille her blode,   *Because*
Over a bacine fair and gode   *basin*
2310   Her throtes he schar atuo.   *Their; cut*
And when he hadde hem bothe slain,
He laid hem in her bed ogain —
No wonder thei him were wo —   *though*
And hilde hem, that no wight schuld se,   *covered*
2315   As noman hadde at hem be;
Out of chaumber he gan go.

And when he was out of chaumber gon,
The dore he steked stille anon   *fastened*
As fast as it was biforn;
2320   The kays he hidde under a ston   *keys*
And thought thai schuld wene ichon   *everyone should think*

That thai hadde ben forlorn.   *murdered*
To his brother he went him than
And seyd to that careful man,
2325   "Swiche time as God was born,
Ich have the brought mi childer blod,
Ich hope it schal do the gode
As the angel seyd biforn."

       "Brother," Sir Amiloun gan to say,
2330   "Hastow slayn thine children tuay?
Allas, whi destow so?"   *did you*
He wepe and seyd, "Waileway!
Ich hat lever til domesday   *would have preferred*
Have lived in care and wo!"
2335   Than seyd Sir Amis, "Be now stille;
Jhesu, when it is His wille,
May send me childer mo.
For me of blis thou art al bare;
Ywis, mi liif wil y nought spare,
2340   To help the now therfro."

       He tok that blode, that was so bright,
And alied that gentil knight,   *anointed*
That er was hend in hale,   *before*
And seththen in bed him dight
2345   And wreighe him wel warm, aplight,   *covered*
With clothes riche and fale.   *many*
"Brother," he seyd, "ly now stille   *lie*
And falle on slepe thurch Godes wille,
As the angel told in tale;
2350   And ich hope wele withouten lesing,   *falsehood*
Jhesu, that is heven king,
Schal bote the of thi bale."   *relieve; trouble*

       Sir Amis let him ly alon   *lie alone*
And in to his chapel he went anon,
2355   In gest as ye may here,
And for his childer, that he hadde slon,
To God of heven he made him mon   *lament*
And preyd with rewely chere   *rueful demeanor*
Schuld save him fram schame that day,
2360   And Mari, his moder, that best may,   *maiden*
That was him leve and dere;
And Jhesu Crist, in that stede   *instance*
Ful wele He herd that knightes bede   *request*
And graunt him his praiere.

2365	Amorwe astite as it was day,	
	The levedi com home al with play	
	With knightes ten and five;	
	Thai sought the kays ther thai lay;	*keys*
	Thai founde hem nought, thai were oway,	
2370	Wel wo was hem olive.	
	The douk bad al that ther wes	
	Thai schuld hold hem still in pes	*peace*
	And stint of her strive,	*cease; anxiety*
	And seyd he hadde the keys nome,	*taken*
2375	Schuld noman in the chaumber come	
	Bot himself and his wive.	

Anon he tok his levedi than
And seyd to hir, "Leve leman,   *Dear beloved*
Be blithe and glad of mode;
2380   For bi Him that this warld wan,
Bothe mi childer ich have slan,   *slain*
That were so hende and gode;
For me thought in mi sweven
That an angel com fram heven
2385   And seyd me thurch her blode   *their blood*
Mi brother schuld passe out of his wo;
Therfore y slough hem bothe to,   *slew*
To hele that frely fode."   *heal; noble young man*

Than was the levedi ferly wo   *terribly grieved*
2390   And seighe hir lord was also;   *saw*
Sche comfort him ful yare,   *fairly*
"O lef liif," sche seyd tho,   *dear; then*
"God may sende ous childer mo,
Of hem have thou no care.
2395   Yif it ware at min hert rote,   *root*
For to bring thi brother bote,   *relief*
My lyf y wold not spare.
Shal noman oure children see,
Tomorow shal they beryed bee
2400   As they faire ded ware!"   *naturally*

Thus the lady faire and bryght
Comfort hur lord with al hur myght,
As ye mow understonde;
And seth they went both ful ryght   *then*
2405   To Sir Amylion, that gentil knyght,
That ere was free to fonde.   *generous in taking on adventures*
When Sir Amylion wakyd thoo,   *then*
Al his fowlehed was agoo   *foulness; gone*

Through grace of Goddes sonde;   *messenger*
2410   Than was he as feire a man
As ever he was yet or than,   *before or then*
Seth he was born in londe.   *Since*

Than were they al blith,   *joyful*
Her joy couth noman kyth,   *understand*
2415   They thonked God that day.
As ye mow listen and lyth,   *hear*
Into a chamber they went swyth,   *quickly*
Ther the children lay;
Without wemme and wound   *blemish*
2420   Hool and sound the children found,   *Whole*
And layen togeder and play.
For joye they wept, there they stood,
And thanked God with myld mood,
Her care was al away.

2425   When Sir Amylion was hool and fere
And wax was strong of powere
Both to goo and ryde,
Child Oweys was a bold squyer,
Blithe and glad he was of chere,
2430   To serve his lord beside.
Than saide the knyght uppon a day,
He wolde hoom to his contray,
To speke with his wyf that tyde;
And for she halp him so at nede,
2435   Wel he thought to quyte hur mede,
No lenger wold he abyde.

Sir Amys sent ful hastely
After mony knyght hardy,
That doughty were of dede,
2440   Wel fyve hundred kene and try,   *proven*
And other barons by and by
On palfray and on steede.
He preked both nyght and day   *galloped*
Til he com to his contray,
2445   Ther he was lord in lede.   *Where; lord over his people*
Than had a knyght of that contré
Spoused his lady, bryght of ble,   *Espoused; countenance*
In romaunce as we rede.

But thus, in romaunce as y yow say,
2450   They com hoom that silf day   *same*
That the bridal was hold;   *wedding*

To the gates they preked without delay,   *galloped*
Anon ther began a soory play
Among the barouns bold.
2455   A messengere to the hal com
And seide her lord was com hom
As man meriest on molde.   *earth*
Than wox the lady blew and wan;   *grew; ashen; pale*
Ther was mony a sory man,
2460   Both yong and olde.

Sir Amys and Sir Amylion
And with hem mony a stout baron
With knyghtes and squyers fale,   *many*
With helmes and with haberyon,   *jacket of mail*
2465   With swerd bryght and broun,
They went in to the hale.
Al that they there araught,   *reached*
Grete strokes there they caught,
Both grete and smale.
2470   Glad and blyth were they that day,
Who so myght skape away   *escape*
And fle fro that bredale.   *wedding feast*

When thei had with wrake   *vengeance*
Drove oute both broun and blake
2475   Out of that worthy woon,   *dwelling*
Sir Amylyon for his lady sake
And grete logge he let make   *lodging had made*
Both of lym and stoon.   *mortar (lime) and stone*
Thereyn was the lady ladde   *led*
2480   And with bred and water was she fed,
Tyl her lyvedays were goon.   *life-days*
Thus was the lady brought to dede,   *death*
Who therof rought, he was a queede,   *cared; bad person*
As ye have herd echoon.

2485   Then Sir Amylion sent his sond   *messenger*
To erles, barouns, fre and bond,
Both feire and hende.
When they com, he sesed in hond   *(see note to line 1508)*
Child Oweys in al his lond,
2490   That was trew and kynde;
And when he had do thus, ywys,
With his brother, Sir Amys,
Agen then gan he wende.
In muche joy without stryf

2495 Togeder ladde they her lyf,
  Tel God after her dide send. *Until*

  Anoon the hend barons tway,
  They let reyse a faire abbay *had built; abbey*
  And feffet it ryght wel thoo, *endowed; then*
2500 In Lumbardy, in that contray,
  To senge for hem tyl Domesday *sing; Judgment Day*
  And for her eldres also. *their parents*
  Both on oo day were they dede
  And in oo grave were they leide, *laid*
2505 The knyghtes both twoo;
  And for her trewth and her godhede
  The blisse of hevyn they have to mede, *for reward*
  That lasteth ever moo.

  Amen

❦ NOTES TO *AMIS AND AMILOUN*

I have used the following abbreviations in these textual and explanatory notes: **A**: Auchinleck Manuscript; **D**: Bodleian Manuscript; **E**: Egerton Manuscript, **H**: Harley Manuscript; **HS**: Lillian Herlands Hornstein in J. Burke Severs, *A Manual of the Writings in Middle English*; **K**: Eugen Kölbing, ed., *Amis and Amiloun*; **L**: MacEdward Leach, ed., *Amis and Amiloun*; **W**: Henry Weber, ed., *Metrical Romances*.

I have based my text on A except that the beginning (lines 1–52) and the end (lines 2441–2508) are lost. Following W and L, I have supplied these lines from E. A has incomplete or damaged versions of lines 53–96, but I have used E for these lines for the sake of ease of reading, unless the fragmentary A version is overwhelmingly persuasive. For a full discussion of the manuscripts see L, who lists all variant readings in all manuscripts. Although L is the definitive critical edition, I have adopted his emendations, suggested in footnotes, only when there would be confusion in reading the text if I did not. I have expanded contractions and corrected obvious scribal errors without comment.

2   *hend(e)* has a variety of meanings: gracious, courteous, lovely, nearby, skillful, and others. It is probably just a polite form of address here.

5   *of.* Omitted in E, it appears in D and H and is adopted by L.

9   *toun and toure.* One of a number of common formulas in the poem like *wele and wo, bryght in bour, lef ne lothe, proude in pride, for soth without lesying,* and *worthy in wede.* See Ford, "New Conception of Poetic Formulae," for more information on formulaic structures throughout this text.

13   *gan*: "began to" or "did" as an auxiliary is common throughout the poem. Similarly, *lete* is often used as an auxiliary meaning "cause to do."

14   *unkouth . . . of kynd.* I have glossed this line "unaffected by their lineage," i.e., "not proud or haughty." L prefers Rickert's "they were not kin," though he does so without conviction and also mentions (without citation) Weston: "their kinsmen knew them not," and Kölbing: "extraordinary they were in character" or "what unknown ancestry they were" (p. 113).

20   *trouth plyght.* The pledging of such an oath of loyalty was a serious matter and probably implied exclusivity in the deepest bond of friendship (cf. lines 361–72). The phrase is often used of marriage or betrothal vows (MED). See Ford, "Merry Married Brothers," for more information on this vow and the paired cups (lines 255–52).

25   Here and elsewhere L cites relations of the English text to French versions.

30   *worthy were in wede*. Variations on this formula are common in this poem.

58   E: *twel yere olde*; A: *twelve winter old*. The use of "winter" better suits the poem's overall tendency to use alliteration.

59   E: *were noon so bold*; A: *was ther non hold*. Although E is grammatically correct, A seems to provide a smoother progression for the sentence as a whole.

61   E: *y*; A: *ich*. I have left E's reading for purposes of consistency within this section. Later, when A becomes the base, I use A's more common form: *ich*.

64   E omits *sende* and finishes the line *his honde*; A: *sende his sonde*. A makes such good sense that I have followed L in substituting A for E.

65   *fre and bond*. This formula depends on the distinction between freemen (and nobles) who held their land in permanent tenure as opposed to bondmen who held land under some form of feudal obligation. *Erles, Barouns* are capitalized in the manuscript, though not consistently elsewhere (e.g., line 86).

73   E: *of*; L follows H: *and*, which seems to make more sense. A is missing this segment of the line.

73–74 A has only the second halves of these lines and has them in reverse order. Like L, I see no reason to disturb E, which is being used as the base for this section of the poem.

76   E: *comyn*; A: *samned*. I have used A because it is more precise, "gathered," and does no violence to the rest of the E line.

79   A: *aplyght*; E: *pyght*. Although A is arguable, I, like L, use *pyght*, "adorned," because it makes better sense in this physical description.

91–96 Ford argues in "Contrasting the Identical" that, despite their apparent similarities, Amiloun is portrayed as the more masculine and Amis as the more feminine throughout the tale.

97   A becomes the base text at this line.

101   A repeats line 98; I have followed L in using E.

120   *proude in pride*. This formula occurs frequently and can be variously rendered as "proud in their pride," "proud in honor," or "in their pride."

188   *botelere*. Although the word can refer simply to a chief servant in charge of dispensing food and drink, the office granted Amis is more likely "A nobleman of the royal court having various duties, including that of supervising the king's buttery and that of acting as royal cupbearer on ceremonial occasions" (MED).

189   A repeats line 186; I have followed L in using the E, H reading.

191   *chef steward in halle*. L quite rightly rejects K's association of *halle* with the place of appointment and instead considers "steward in halle" as a special office which

involved overall management of the affairs of the castle and was ordinarily held by a noble.

231   *God me spede*. Here and in line 300 this phrase has the sense of the modern vernacular "God help me."

244   *goldsmithe*. A: *goldsmiþe*. A scribal efficiency, whereby the *þ* is made by a loop following *t* that leads in a single stroke to *e*.

280   *herkneth*. L reads *hekeneþ* here and in lines 517 and 1189.

296   A: *faily*; I have preferred E: *faile*.

314   A: *Amis*; E, D, H: *Amylioun*. Amis is clearly the wrong character; L follows E, D, H. I have emended to "Amiloun," the more common spelling in A.

334   *bright in bour*: literally "beautiful in bower," a common formula in this poem.

350   Stewards in medieval literature were notorious for treachery. See the false stewards in *Havelok*, Gower's *Confessio Amantis* II, 2496–2781, and the treacherous stewardship of Mordred in the *Alliterative Morte Arthure*. It is no wonder that Orfeo in *Sir Orfeo* takes precautions upon his return to see that his steward has been faithful.

361   These lines echo Amiloun's parting words (lines 308 ff.).

365   *to the*. Only found in A. Omitted in the other MSS. L deletes.

389   Strictly speaking, Amis is not a traitor since he has not broken an oath to the steward.

395   *slo*. Literally a sloeberry; since "not giving a sloe" is no longer idiomatic, I have glossed the line: "don't give a fig."

398   *wrethe*. A: *wretþe*. Also in lines 404, 718, 830, 1092, 1213, 1322, and 1785. A scribal efficiency. Similarly *wrethi* in line 606 is spelled *wretþi* in A. See note to line 244.

438   *halle*. L emends to *hale*, on the witness of E, thus improving the eye-rhyme with *tale* and *sale*.

448   *mirie*. L: *miri*.

478   A adds *with him* after *might*, an eye-skip from the following line.

487   *com*. L reads as *come* here and in lines 1549 and 2153. A, W, and K read *com*.

505   The episode that begins here contains both the familiar "love temptation" in a garden and the conventional "love-longing" of the courtly love tradition.

550–51   The sense of these lines, a bit confusing because of Middle English use of negatives, is that she would for no one hesitate to make her way to him.

617   A canon was an ordained clergyman who was not under monastic rule, usually attached to a cathedral or church (MED).

645   *drawe*. Amis fears that, if he succumbs and the duke finds out, he will be executed and "drawe," dragged behind horses — neither a cruel nor unusual punishment for such a breach of fidelity and chastity.

686   *des* (dais): "The place occupied by a king, councillors, judges, etc." (MED).

721–23   In medieval romance, a preferred time for sexual intrigue is often when the lord is away hunting. See the *Stanzaic Morte Arthur* and *Sir Gawain and the Green Knight*.

726   *Sche went, as sche wele kan*. In a note L prefers some version of E, D, H: *Wel right the way sche nam*. *Kan* is, however, a legitimate past form of *connen*: "to have the ability to do something" (MED).

758   *Seyn Tomas of Ynde*. In John 21:25 ff., doubting Thomas placed his hand in the wound in Christ's side, thus proving His resurrected corporeality. According to saints' lore, Thomas proselytized in India, was martyred and buried. Stories about him abound. In one legend he opens Mary's tomb to see if she is still there. When he finds her body gone, he looks up and beholds it ascending. She drops him her girdle (a sign of chastity), thereby affirming the Assumption. Mandeville claims to have visited Thomas' tomb in India (*Travels*, ch. 20) where the Apostle's hand is kept in a separate vessel and used to make just assessments of hard cases: the hand casts aside false claims and clings to the just. It is fitting that the maiden Belisaunt calls upon Thomas as she chastises Amis for his doubts about her love: *Whi seystow ever nay?* (line 759).

768   L supplies *she*. The word is needed, but I have followed E, H: *sche*.

771   *hem for to here*. I have followed E by inserting *Their consail* at the beginning of the line.

785   It was common in romances to swear by saints, though here St. John the Apostle is especially popular. See lines 832, 956, 1918, 2161. Ford argues that the saints' lives invoked throughout this text are simply variations on a formula used to fit different rhyme, meter, and alliterative needs, but have no special meanings ("New Conception of Poetic Formulae," pp. 218–24).

796   St. James the Greater, whose body is said to be buried at Compostela, Spain, which consequently became a major pilgrimage site. There does not, however, seem to be any special significance here for Saint James, just as there does not seem to be elsewhere for St. Thomas of Inde (line 758), St. Giles (lines 952, 1126), St. Denis of France (line 1567), or St. Martin (line 2014).

835–40   The sense is that, if anyone has lied about him and the duke's daughter, he (Amis) will challenge the lie by combat.

849   *Ataint* implies conviction of a serious crime subject to the death penalty or loss of civil or property rights (OED).

860   An ambiguous line. L observes that Rickert believes the daughter is speaking in this line and translates "among" as "before" but that H "rather confirms the reading: and her mother swore continually (ever among)."

872   In medieval law a "borwe" was someone who offered himself as a surety or
           guarantee for someone else's appearance at court. If the charge was a capital
           offense, the guarantor might forfeit his life (MED). Thus, threats are made later
           to burn the "borwes." Note also the difficulty Guinevere has in getting guar-
           antors when she is accused of killing the Scottish knight in the *Stanzaic Morte
           Arthur* (lines 1328 ff.).

939   A: *wrorth*; E: *wroth* (accepted by L and me).

950   A: *no nother*, but I emended to *non other*, an obvious false juncture.

952   *Seyn Gile*. A hermit saint who founded the monastery in Provence, bearing his
           name. The place became an important pilgrimage center on the routes to
           Compostela and the Holy Land. There were several English festivals honoring
           him as well. His patronage was thought to be beneficial to travelers, cripples,
           lepers, and mothers in childbearing. Amis calls upon Saint Gile as he sets out to
           help Amiloun, little aware of the multiple role that the saint could play in his life
           as he becomes crippled with leprosy that may be cured only with a baby's blood.

984   *Waileway*. An interjection of lament, a "woe is me" or "woe the day" sentiment.

988   L explains that knights wore long coats that had to be tucked up for walking or
           riding (p. 123).

1054   L supplies *a* for a letter in A that looks like *r*.

1077   *sorn*. K defines as "scorn"; L prefers "mockery" from French *sorne*. I prefer MED:
           "grief, sorrow, distress, trouble, harm." MED cites *Guy of Warwick* as well as *Amis
           and Amiloun*. The word also appears in line 2141.

1109–10   Judas sold (betrayed) Christ for "thirty pieces of silver." Christ died "on Rode"
           (on the Cross), thereby redeeming mankind from Adam and Eve's sin. Similar
           references are common in this and other medieval poems.

1164   The sword lying between a man and a woman, as a sign of chastity, is common,
           as in various tales of Tristan and Isolde. See L, p. lxiii.

1176   A: *wardles*; E: *worldes*. I read *warldes*, which appears elsewhere in the poem and
           is a simple transposition of *d* and *l* in A.

1217   The *tonne* (barrel) was apparently meant to conceal their nakedness — an odd
           delicacy of feeling under the circumstances.

1252   *And sayd*. A: *say*. K emends to *And sayd*, followed by L and me. W reads *Stay*.

1253   *passioun*: Christ's passion is comprised of His last sufferings and culminates in
           the Crucifixion.

1290   Each participant in the combat had to swear an oath as to the truth of his cause;
           the winner was vindicated.

1339   *That*. A: *The*. K's emendation, followed by L and me. W follows A.

1456   *unkende*: possibly "unnatural" or "untaught" (L); more likely here "different
           from her kind (family)."

1508	*sesed*: "put in legal or formal possession (of a kingdom, land, feudal estate, goods, etc.)" (MED).
1511	Of course, Belisent (Belisaunt) is not, strictly speaking, a maiden at this point.
1540–45	Here Amiloun is being punished for pretending to be Amis in the "ordeal." Leprosy was often seen in medieval literature as a punishment by God and frequently used as a metaphor for moral corruption. See Saul N. Brody, *The Disease of the Soul: Leprosy in Medieval Literature* (Ithaca: Cornell University Press, 1974).
1546	*In gest to rede*. The "geste," which is the narrator's source, is probably one of the Anglo-Norman versions of the tale or an English redaction of an Anglo-Norman source. The story was ubiquitous in both romance and hagiographic versions. See L, pp. ix–cii. The narrator frequently refers to his "gest" or "book" or "romance," but no specific identification of the source has been made.
1567	Saint Denis (also known as Dionysius) is popularly known as the patron saint of France, and legend has it that he carried his severed head to the location where his abbey church was to be built.
1568	A: *Te*; I have followed L in preferring E, D: *The*.
1653	The five wounds of Christ were from the nails in his hands and feet and the spear in his side.
1678	A: *wrorn*; I follow L in preferring E, D: *sworn*.
1711	*messais*, meaning "suffering from starvation," "hungry," "needy," "wretched," "feeble," "miserable," etc. See MED *misese* and its variant spellings. L and K read *messaner* without conjecture as to the meaning.
1769	A: *mensenger*. Like L, I have followed E, D: *messanger*.
1771	*praieste*: probably a Northern form of *praieth the* (L). The sense of the lines 1769–73 is "He sent me as a messanger because he cannot walk and begs you to send him enough of his goods to buy an ass to ride on."
1816	*hem*. L: *him*.
1864	*cité toun*. A town became a city if it had a cathedral.
2008	*gold*. A: *glod*. Emended by all.
2014	Saint Martin, known as Martin of Tours, was a soldier who refused to kill Christians. The popular story about St. Martin is that he split his cloak with a naked beggar. This is significant because Amis is, at the time of this oath, instructing his servant to do an act of charity for the begging leper, Amiloun.
2113-24	This stanza is omitted in A. These lines correspond to D lines 2012–24.
2136	*that*. Reduplicated in A.
2206	A: *childer*; like L, I have followed E, D: *brother*.
2209-20	This stanza is omitted in E, D.

2226	*care*. A reads *wo*, which is crossed out, and *care* is added in the margin in another hand.
2242	A: *min*; like L, I have followed E, D: *thin*.
2293	*hadde*. A: *hadde hadde* with the second *hadde* deleted.
2397	The rest of the text is from E, following L and the advice of HS.
2399	*Tomorow* as in E. L reads *Tomorrow*.
2405	A has this variant spelling of *Amiloun* here and in lines 2407 and 2425. E has it in 2461, 2485. E has *Amylyon* at 2476.
2424	E: *agoo*; like L, I have followed D: *away*, which maintains the rhyme.
2442	*steede*. L reads *steed*.
2472–74	Omitted in E; I have followed L in using D.

❧ INTRODUCTION TO *ROBERT OF CISYLE*

Although it is characteristic of romance to concentrate on the experience and values of one hero (or two, as in *Amis and Amiloun*), in *Robert of Cisyle* the focus on Robert is especially intense. It is his experience as he falls from high position, is punished, and rises again that is the whole substance of the poem. All other characters, even the angel who temporarily replaces him as king, are there only for our understanding of Robert and the meaning of his experiences.

The story was common and popular: there are ten manuscript versions of *Robert of Cisyle*. The theme appears in the Bible and folklore as well as romance: that the mighty will be brought low and the humble exalted. The most prominent biblical statement of the theme is the Magnificat, Mary's speech to Elizabeth revealing that she has conceived the Redeemer, which is partially quoted in the poem:

Deposuit potentes de sede,	*He hath put down the mighty from their seat,*
Et exaltavit humiles.	*And hath exalted the humble.*
(lines 40–41)	

The theme is pious and didactic — and comforting to a popular audience who can enjoy the fall of the great as well as the ultimate triumph of the hero once he has been thoroughly humiliated. That is the double enjoyability of *Robert of Cisyle*: in the fall of the mighty, so common in medieval tragedy (see, for example, the Monk's compendium in *The Canterbury Tales*), there is a didactic caution to "all of us." In romance versions, however, the fall and rise is doubly satisfying since we can observe the punishment of arrogance and the reward for humility which links the hero to "people like us."

The didactic point is sharpened by the insistent concentration on Robert, his position, his suffering, his remorse, and his restoration. Robert does not even have a wife. He begins as a good king of great family: one brother is Pope Urban, the other is the Holy Roman Emperor Valemounde. There is a temptation because of the specificity to find an historical model, but, although there were two popes Urban who might fit the bill, there is no precedent for the trial and, indeed, no Holy Roman Emperor named Valemounde (although his made-up name is suggestive since it means "farewell to the world," a version of *contemptus mundi* that Robert must learn in order to regain his kingdom). The importance of his brothers is just that — their importance. Robert is king of a prosperous Sicily and the brother of the two most powerful men in the Christian world. If he can be laid low, who is not vulnerable? This heightens the doubled joy of this romance. Even Robert can be humbled by God and even the sinful can be restored through genuine repentance.

At the outset it is made clear that he is high-born, the flower of chivalry:

> In Cisyle was a noble kyng,   *Sicily*
> Fair and strong and sumdel yyng.   *somewhat young*
>   (lines 3–4)

The opening descriptions are abstract and laudatory; his youth may even mitigate to some extent the foolishness of his pride, though if that is the case it is one of the few mercies the poet allows Robert. More prominent is his arrogance:

> The kyng thoughte, he hedde no peer   *had*
> In al the worlde, fer no neer;
> And in his thought he hedde pryde,
> For he was nounpeer in uch a syde.   *arbiter (judge) on either side*
>   (lines 25–28)

His arrogance even extends, ominously, to matters of religion:

> He thoughte more in worldes honour,   *cared more about*
> Than in Crist, ur saveour.   *our savior*
>   (lines 33–34)

When he is at vespers and hears the Magnificat he must ask for a translation:

> He made a clerk hit him rehers   *repeat*
> In langage of his owne tonge,
> In Latyn he nuste, that heo songe.   *He did not know Latin*
>   (lines 36–38)

Although his ignorance of Latin may soften some of the sharp edges of his personality for a popular audience, it also identifies him as an outsider who does not understand the language of the Church. When he hears the translation his reaction is not merely arrogant but blasphemous; he directly challenges the truth of Scripture:

> "Al your song is fals and fable!   *false*
> What mon hath such pouwer,   *man; power*
> Me to bringe lowe in daunger?"   *danger*
>   (lines 50–52)

And this challenge is explicitly chastised by the narrator: "This errour he hedde in thought" (line 58). Thus, he is so self-absorbed as to blind himself to the necessary truth of Scripture. This is a serious error, because revelation must be true even if it does not seem to be borne out in our own experience thus far. He is also so bored as to fall asleep. Robert's nap during vespers has consequences harsher than the ordinary experience of most drowsy worshippers because of his high position and because it is a metaphor for his indifference to the word of God.

That he is not recognized by the guards when he awakes after the service is not simply a convenience of romance but a sign that his obstinacy in the face of revealed truth has made him unrecognizable even by his own retainers. The angel who takes his form and place is easily accepted because he is an idealized version of Robert; he is Robert at his best. He is received joyously by the people while the fallen Robert is seized as a potential robber.

Here again the poem is metaphorical and didactic. Robert at his best is angelic; Robert in defiance of Scripture is indeed a spiritual thief. When his asseverations of his identity are rejected by the porter and he is excluded from his own palace, he is displayed as someone who has put himself outside of the Christian community. His ferocity when he is rejected may not be more than one would expect of a confident king, but it is certainly presented as a sign of his failure to understand the limitations on the prerogatives of human power:

> "Thou schalt witen, ar I go: *know, before*
> Thi kyng I am; thow schalt knowe.
> In prison thou schalt ligge lowe   *lie*
> And ben anhonged and todrawe   *be hanged and pulled to pieces*
> As a traytur bi the lawe.   *traitor according to the law*
> Thou schalt wel witen, I am kyng,   *know*
> Open the gates, gadelyng!"
>   (lines 98–104)

His attempts to justify and identify himself by his family are tellingly futile:

> "The Pope of Roome is my brother
> And the emperour myn other."   *my*
>   (lines 149–50)

When the porter reports his encounter with Robert, the angel-king uses the word "fool" for the first time to refer to Robert, and this becomes the dominant metaphor for his outcast situation throughout the rest of the poem:

> "Thou art a fol, that art nought fert   *fool; afraid*
> Mi men to don such vilenye."   *do; villainy*
>   (lines 142–43)

Spiritually foolish, Robert is in fact made into a "king's fool":

> "Thow art my fol," seide the angel,   *fool*
> "Thou schal be schoren everichdel,   *shaved completely*
> Lych a fool, a fool to be . . ."   *Like*
>   (lines 153–55)

His relationship to animals, apes, and dogs establishes a new position for him in the hierarchy of creation. The irony is intensified by the fact that his assayer (royal food taster) will be a dog and not only will he be bestial (he might learn from an ape), but he will have to contend with the dogs for his food. Unlike the title character in *Sir Gowther*, who also is a "fool" and must eat under the table with the dogs, Robert is not undergoing the transformation from "wild man" to knight that Gowther is. Robert has been moved dramatically downward in the chain of being. Robert does not accept his humiliation easily, yet it is always clear that he has no choice. The narrator is sympathetic, but he does not justify Robert: his humiliation is painfully described, but we are told clearly that the angel-king ruled well.

Bad becomes even worse when, after three years of rule by the angel-king, Valemounde issues an invitation for the three brothers to get together in Rome. The invitation, coming at this point, only makes sense within the narrator's logic of romance: it is motivated by the development of theme rather than any internal necessity of plot; it is intended to make humiliation even more humiliating. The angel-king goes, clad in brilliant white (Robert at his best), and is joyfully greeted by his "brothers." Robert goes along as the king's fool and, despite his protestations, is perceived as the fool that he is both literally and figuratively:

Tho was he more fol iholde,	*Therefore; fool considered*
More then er a thousend folde;	*before; times*
To cleyme such a bretherhede:	*claim; brotherhood*
Hit was holde a foles dede.	*considered; fool's deed*
(lines 289–92)	

He goes wild with grief when he is rejected by his brothers:

"Allas," quath he, "nou am I lowe."	*said*
For he hopede, bi eny thing,	*hoped, somehow*
His bretheren wolde ha mad hym kyng;	*brothers; have*
And whon his hope was al ago,	*when; gone*
He seide "allas" and "weilawo."	*alas; wellaway*
(lines 296–300)	

It is, however, this ultimate rejection by his potent brothers that occasions Robert's renovation, poignantly introduced by his "allas" in line 307. He here begins a series of recognitions, not just of his situation but of his interior disposition. He thinks of the biblical example of Nebuchadnezzar, who was brought low even though Holofernes had thought of him as a "god." Despite the fact that the biblical basis of the exemplum is scanty, it is significant that Robert's first recognition comes through Scripture, the rejection of which had been the narrative turning point in his own fortunes.

Robert eventually applies the story to himself, accepts his guilt, and admits his pride:

"Now am I wel lowe ipult,	*brought down*
And that is right that I so be."	
(lines 346–47)	

Many casual critics of the poem (few have dealt with it intensively) have dismissed the narrative as "sprawling" and "simplistic." Such commentators should pay particular attention to the lyrical self-conviction that follows this fundamental recognition; the next twenty-four lines are devoted to a graceful revelation, by Robert himself, of his transgressions. He prays to Mary (and to God) to forgive him for his culpable foolishness. It is particularly appropriate that this admission insist on the metaphor of the fool that recurs throughout his confession as a refrain: "Lord, on Thi fool Thow have pité" (line 348). He explicitly cites his rejection of Scripture and lists his trespasses. He accepts his "fooldom" and generalizes it to the human condition. He prays to Mary for the very humility he is now displaying: his recognition is interior and total. Since we are "in a romance" we have every reason to expect that the consequences will be salubrious — and they are.

The angel accepts Robert's self-abasement and reinforces the lesson by restoring him, while explaining that one hour in heaven brings more joy than one hundred thousand years as a noble man on earth. Having underlined the point, the angel disappears and Robert, morally chastened and spiritually elevated, returns to his exalted role with a critical new awareness of where even the mighty fit into the great scheme of God's universe. When he regains power, he rules as a better king than ever. Why he, a "yyng" man (line 4), should die within two years is left unexplained; perhaps the kingdom of heaven is all that is left for his exaltation. Appropriately, upon his death, he lets his story be known as a lesson to his people and to the world.

In any case the lesson is clear and is reiterated: the mighty will be brought low and the humble exalted. The pious conclusion, which refers both to Christ's redemptive act and to the experience of the individual Christian, invites, more explicitly than is usual in romance, a fourfold allegorical interpretation. Literally, this is the story of the experience of the king of Sicily. Allegorically, it is the expression of the human condition within the divinely shaped hierarchy of the created world: human pride can expect a fall, while humility will bring rewards. Analogically, it is the story of Christ's self-abasement in his acceptance of the pain and humiliation of crucifixion for the salvation of mankind. Anagogically, it is advice to all Christians on what is necessary for salvation. *Robert of Cisyle* certainly is didactic, but it is not a slender or careless redundancy. It is a lively, powerful, and sometimes charmingly playful statement of a fundamental and gratifying Christian principle.

Select Bibliography

Manuscripts

Bodleian 3938, English Poetry A.1 (Vernon), at the Bodleian Library, Oxford University. Fols. 300r–301r. [c. 1390. 444 lines.]

Trinity Oxford D. 57, at Trinity College, Oxford University. Fols. 165r–167r. [c. 1380–1400. 440 lines.]

Cambridge University Ff.2.38 (formerly More 690), at the Cambridge University Library. Fols. 254r–257v. [late fifteenth to early sixteenth century. 516 lines.]

Cambridge University Ii.4.9., at the Cambridge University Library. Fols. 87v–93v. [late fifteenth century. 374 lines.]

Caius Cambridge 174, at Gonville and Caius College, Cambridge University. Pp. 456–68. [late fifteenth century. 470 lines.]

BM Harley 525, at the British Library, London. Fols. 35r–43v. [mid- to late fifteenth century. 472 lines.]

BM Harley 1701 (formerly Harley Plutarch 1701), at the British Library, London. Fols. 92–95. [c. 1380. 476 lines.]

BM Additional 22283 (Simeon), at the British Library, London. Fols. 90v–91v. [c. 1390–1400. 444 lines.]

BM Additional 34801, at the British Library, London. Fol. 2. [c. 1417–32. 23 lines.]

Trinity Dublin 432 B, at Trinity College, Dublin. Fols. 60r–61v. [after 1461. 79 lines.]

Editions

The Vernon Manuscript: A Facsimile of Bodleian Library, Oxford, MS. Eng. Poet. a.1. With introduction by A. I. Doyle. Cambridge: D. S. Brewer, 1987.

Horstmann, Carl, ed. *Sammlung Altenglischer Legenden*. Heilbronn: Henninger, 1878. Pp. 209–19.

Nuck, Robert, ed. *Roberd of Cisyle*. Berlin: Bernstein, 1887.

French, Walter Hoyt, and Charles Brockway Hale, eds. *Middle English Metrical Romances*. New York: Prentice-Hall, 1930. Pp. 931–46.

Criticism

Baker, Joan. "*Deposuit potentes*: Apocalptic Rhetoric in the Middle English *Robert of Sicily*." *Medieval Perspectives* (1997), 25–45.

Harper, Stephen. *Insanity, Individuals, and Society in Late-Medieval English Literature: The Subject of Madness*. Lewiston, NY: Edwin Mellen Press, 2003.

Hopkins, Andrea. "Roberd of Cisyle." In *The Sinful Knights: A Study of Middle English Penitential Romance*. Oxford: Clarendon Press, 1990. Pp. 179–95.

Hornstein, Lillian Herlands. "*King Robert of Sicily*: Analogues and Origins." *PMLA* 79 (1964), 13–21.

Olsen, Alexandra Hennessey. "Oral Tradition in the Middle English Romance: The Case of Robert of Cisyle." In *Oral Poetics in Middle English Poetry*. Ed. Mark C. Amodio. New York: Garland, 1994. Pp. 71–87.

———. "The Return of the King: A Reconsideration of *Robert of Sicily*." *Folklore* 93 (1982), 216–19.

Powell, Stephen D. "Multiplying Textuality: Generic Migration in the Manuscripts of *Roberd of Cisyle*." *Anglia* 116 (1998), 171–97.

Simons, John. "A Byzantine Identity for *Robert of Cisyle*." In *The Matter of Identity in Medieval Romance*. Ed. Phillipa Hardman. Cambridge: D. S. Brewer, 2002. Pp. 103–11.

ROBERT OF CISYLE

	Princes proude that beth in pres,	*proud; in company*
	I wol you telle thing, not lees!	*lies*
	In Cisyle was a noble kyng,	*Sicily*
	Fair and strong and sumdel yyng.	*somewhat young*
5	He hedde a brother in grete Roome,	*had*
	Pope of alle Cristendome;	*Christendom*
	Another he hedde in Alemayne,	*had; Germany*
	An Emperour, that Sarazins wroughte payne.	*pain [upon] Saracens*
	The kyng was hote kyng Robert,	*named*
10	Never man ne wiste him fert;	*No one ever knew him to be afraid*
	He was kyng of gret honour	
	For that he was conquerour;	
	In al the world nas his peer,	*was not his equal*
	Kyng ne prince, fer no neer.	*far or near*
15	And, for he was of chivalrie flour,	*flower of chivalry*
	His brother was mad Emperour,	*made*
	His other brother Godes vikere,	*vicar*
	Pope of Rome, as I seide ere.	*before*
	The pope was hote pope Urban,	
20	He was good to God and man;	
	The Emperour was hote Valemounde,	
	A strengur weorreour nas non founde	*stronger warrior was not*
	After his brother of Cisyle,	
	Of whom that I schal telle a while.	
25	The kyng thoughte, he hedde no peer	*had*
	In al the worlde, fer no neer;	
	And in his thought he hedde pryde,	
	For he was nounpeer in uch a syde.	*arbiter (judge) on either side*
	At midsomer, a Seynt Jones Niht,	*on June 24*
30	The kyng to churche com ful riht,	*church; directly*
	Forto heeren his evensong.	*To hear; (see note)*
	Hym thoughte, he dwelled ther ful long:	
	He thoughte more in worldes honour,	*cared more about*
	Than in Crist, ur saveour.	*our savior*
35	In "Magnificat" he herde a vers,	*verse*
	He made a clerk hit him rehers	*repeat*
	In langage of his owne tonge,	

	In Latyn he nuste, that heo songe.	*He did not know Latin*
	The vers was this, I telle the:	
40	Deposuit potentes de sede,	*(see note)*
	Et exaltavit humiles.	
	This was the vers, withouten les.	*lies*
	The clerk seide anone riht;	*right away*
	"Sire, such is Godes miht,	
45	That he may make heyghe lowe	*high*
	And lowe heighe in luytel throwe.	*in an instant*
	God may do, withoute lyghe,	*lie*
	His wil in twynklyng of an eighe."	*eye*
	The kyng seide with herte unstable:	*heart not steadfast (in virtue)*
50	"Al your song is fals and fable!	*false*
	What mon hath such pouwer,	*man; power*
	Me to bringe lowe in daunger?	*danger*
	I am flour of chivalrye,	*flower of chivalry*
	Myn enemys I may distruye;	*destroy*
55	No mon lyveth in no londe,	
	That me may withstonde.	*withstand*
	Then is this a song of nouht!"	
	This errour he hedde in thought.	*had*
	And in his thouht a sleep him tok	*took*
60	In his pulput, as seith the bok.	*royal pew*
	Whon that evensong was al don,	*When; done*
	A kyng ilyk him out gan gon,	*looking like him went out*
	And alle men with hym gan wende,	*went*
	Kyng Robert lafte out of mynde.	*was forgotten*
65	The newe kyng was, as I you telle,	
	Godes angel, his pruide to felle.	*pride; destroy*
	The angel in halle joye made,	
	And alle men of hym weore glade.	*were glad*
	The kyng wakede, that lay in churche,	*waked who*
70	His men he thouhte wo to worche,	*woe (i.e., harm) to work*
	For he was laft ther alon,	*left there alone*
	And derk niht him fel uppon.	*dark*
	He gan crie after his men,	*began to call*
	Ther nas non, that spak agen.	*was none; back*
75	But the sexteyn atten eende	*sexton; at the back*
	Of the churche to him gan wende,	*went*
	And seide: "What dost thou nouthe her,	*now here*
	Thou false thef, thou losenger?	*thief; scoundrel*
	Thou art her with felenye,	*here; evil intent*
80	Holy churche to robbye."	*rob*
	He seide: "Foule gadelyng,	*said; rascal*
	I am no thef, I am a kyng!	*thief*
	Opene the churche dore anon,	*at once*
	That I mowe to mi paleis gon!"	*might go to my palace*

85	The sexteyn thouhte anon with than,	*sexton; thereupon*
	That he was sum wood man,	*mad*
	And wolde the chirche dilyveret were	*wanted the church rid*
	Of hym, for he hedde fere;	*he had fear*
	And openede the chirchedore in haste.	
90	The kyng bygon to renne out faste,	*began to run*
	As a mon that was wood.	*man*
	At his paleys gate he stood,	*palace*
	And heet the porter gadelyng	*called*
	And bad hym come in highing,	*haste*
95	Anon the gates up to do.	*to lift up*
	The porter seide: "Ho clepeth so?"	*Who says*
	He onswerde anon tho:	*answered; then*
	"Thou schalt witen, ar I go:	*know, before*
	Thi kyng I am; thou schalt knowe.	
100	In prison thou schalt ligge lowe	*lie*
	And ben anhonged and todrawe	*be hanged and pulled to pieces*
	As a traytur bi the lawe.	*traitor according to the law*
	Thou schalt wel witen, I am kyng,	*know*
	Open the gates, gadelyng!"	
105	The porter seide: "So mot I the,	*might I thrive*
	The kyng is mid his meyne;	*with his company*
	Wel I wot, withoute doute,	*know*
	The kyng nis not now withoute."	*is not; outside*
	The porter com into halle,	
110	Bifore the newe kyng aknes gan falle	*on his knees*
	And seide: "Ther is atte gate	
	A nyce fool icome late.	*silly fool come recently*
	He seith he is lord and kyng	
	And clept me foule gadelyng.	*called; rascal*
115	Lord, what wol ye that I do?	
	Leten hym in or leten him go?"	*Let*
	The angel seide ryght in haste:	
	"Do him come in swithe faste!	*Have; very quickly*
	For my fol I wole him make,	*fool; will*
120	Forte he the name of kyng forsake."	*Until*
	The porter com to the gate	
	And him he called in to late.	*let*
	He smot the porter, whon he com in,	*struck; when*
	That blod barst out of mouth and chyn.	*burst*
125	The porter yeld him his travayle,	*requited; pains*
	Him smot ageyn, withouten fayle,	*struck back*
	That neose and mouth barst a blood;	*[So] that nose; burst with*
	Thenne he semed almost wod.	*insane*
	The porter and his men in haste,	
130	Kyng Robert in a podel caste;	*puddle*
	Unsemely heo maden his bodi than,	*Unattractive they*

That he nas lyk non other man,   *was not like*
And brouht him bifore the newe kyng;
And seide: "Lord, this gadelyng
135   Me hath smyte withoute decert;   *Has hit me; desert*
He seith, he is ur kyng apert.   *our; openly*
This harlot oughte for his sawe   *vagabond; assertion*
Ben ihonged and todrawe;   *hanged and pulled to pieces*
For he seith non other word,
140   Bote that he is bothe kyng and lord."   *But*
The angel seide to kyng Robert:
"Thou art a fol, that art nought fert   *fool; afraid*
Mi men to don such vilenye;   *do; villainy*
Thi gult thou most nede abuye.   *guilt; atone for*
145   What art thou?" seide the angel.
Qwath Robert: "Thou shalt wite wel,   *Said; know*
That I am kyng and kyng wol be,   *will*
With wronge thou hast my dignité.   *have; worthiness*
The Pope of Roome is my brother
150   And the emperour myn other;   *my*
Heo wol me wreke, for soth to telle,   *They; avenge; truth*
I wot, heo nulle not longe dwelle."   *know; they will not; delay*
"Thow art my fol," seide the angel,   *fool*
"Thou schal be schoren everichdel,   *shaved completely*
155   Lych a fool, a fool to be,   *Like*
Wher is now thi dignité?   *your honor*
Thi counseyler schal ben an ape,   *advisor*
And o clothyng you worth ischape.   *one (same) clothing; shall be dressed*
I schal him clothen as thi brother,
160   Of o clothyng — hit is non other;
He schal beo thin owne feere,   *be; companion*
Sum wit of him thou miht lere.   *learn*
Houndes, how so hit bifalle,   *Hounds; as it will happen*
Schulen eten with the in halle;   *Shall eat*
165   Thou schalt eten on the ground;
Thin assayour schal ben an hound,   *taster*
To assaye thi mete bifore the;   *test; you*
Wher is now thi dignité?"   *dignity*
He heet a barbur hym bifore,   *called*
170   That as a fool he schulde be schore,   *So that; shorn*
Al around lich a frere   *like a friar*
An hondebrede bove either ere,   *hand's width above each ear*
And on his croune made a crois.   *crown (top of his head); cross*
He gan crie and make nois.   *cry out; noise*
175   He swor, thei schulde alle abuye,   *pay for it*
That hym dude such vileynye,   *did; villainy*
And evere he seide he was lord,
And uche mon scorned him for that word,   *each man*

	And uche mon seide he was wod,	*each; mad*
180	That proved wel, he couthe no good.	*showed well; understood [nothing]*
	For he wende in none wyse,	*thought in no way*
	That God Almihti couthe devyse,	*could*
	Him to bringe to lower stat:	*state*
	With o drauht he was chekmat!	*one move; checkmated*
185	With houndes everi niht he lay,	
	And ofte he criyede weylaway,	*cried allas*
	That he evere was ibore,	*born*
	For he was a mon forlore.	*man totally lost*
	Ther nas in court grom ne page,	*was not; groom nor*
190	That of the kyng ne made rage;	*ridicule*
	For no mon ne mihte him knowe,	*no man; recognize*
	He was defygured in a throwe.	*changed in appearance; instant*
	So lowe er that was never kyng;	*before*
	Allas, her was a deolful thing,	*here; mournful*
195	That he scholde for his pryde	
	Such hap among his men betyde!	*fortune; experience*
	Hunger and thurst he hedde grete,	*had great*
	For he ne moste no mete ete,	*could not eat food*
	But houndes eeten of his disch,	
200	Whether hit weore flesch or fisch.	*meat or fish*
	He was to dethe neigh ibrouht	*nearly brought*
	For hunger, ar he miht eten ouht	*before; could; anything*
	With houndes that beth in halle.	
	How might him hardore bifalle?	*How might (anything) harder befall him*
205	And whon hit nolde non other be,	*when it might not be otherwise*
	He eet with houndes gret plenté.	*great plenty*
	The angel was kyng, him thoughte long;	*it seemed to him*
	In his tyme was never wrong,	
	Tricherie, ne falshede, ne no gyle	*Treachery; falsehood; guile*
210	Idon in the lond of Cisyle.	*Done*
	Alle goode ther was gret plenté:	*goods; great plenty*
	Among men, love and charité;	
	In his tyme was never strif	*strife*
	Bitwene mon and his wyf;	*man; wife*
215	Uche mon lovede wel other:	*Each*
	Beter love nas nevere of brother.	*was never between*
	Thenne was that a joyful thing	
	In londe to have such a kyng.	
	Kyng he was threo yeer and more.	*three years*
220	Robert yeode as mon forlore.	*went as man utterly lost*
	Seythe hit fel uppon a day	*Later it happened upon a day*
	A luytel bifore the moneth of May,	*little*
	Sire Valemound, the emperour,	
	Sende lettres of gret honour	*great*
225	To his brother, of Cisyle kyng,	

And bad him come withouten lettyng,   *delay*
That heo mihten beo bothe isome   *they might be; together*
With heore brother, Pope of Rome.   *their*
Hym thoughte long heo weore atwinne;   *it seemed to him; they; apart*
230 He bad him lette for no wynne,   *spare; consideration*
That he neore of good aray   *arrive in good array*
In Roome an Holy Thoresday.   *on Holy Thursday*
The angel welcomede the messagers   *messengers*
And gaf hem clothes riche of Pers,   *gave; from Persia*
235 Furred al with ermyne;   *Trimmed with ermine*
In Cristendom is non so fyne;
And al was chouched mid perré,   *decorated with gems*
Better was non in Cristianté.   *Christendom*
Such cloth, and hit weore to dihte,   *if it had to be made*
240 Al Cristendom hit make ne mihte;   *could not make it*
Of that wondrede al that lond,   *wondered*
Hou that cloth was wrought with hond;   *How; made; hand*
Wher such cloth was to selle,
Ne ho hit maade, couthe no mon telle.   *Who made it, could*
245 The messagers wenten with the kyng   *messengers*
To grete Rome withoute lettyng.   *delay*
The fool Robert also went,
Clothed in lodly garnement,   *hideous garments*
With foxes tayles mony aboute: *tails many*
250 Men miht him knowen in the route.   *recognize; along the way*
The angel was clothed al in whit;   *white*
Nas never seyghe such samyt;   *Was never seen such rich silk*
And al was chouched myd perles riche,   *decorated with pearls*
Never mon seigh none hem liche.   *man saw; like*
255 Al whit atyr was and steede,   *white attire; horse*
The steede was feir, ther he yede;   *horse; on which he went*
So feir a steede, as he on rod,   *rode*
Nas never mon that ever bistrod.   *man; bestrode*
The angel com to Roome sone,   *soon*
260 Real, as fel a kyng to done;   *Royally; was fitting*
So real kyng com never in Rome,   *Such a royal*
Alle men wondrede whethen he come.   *from where*
His men weore realliche diht;   *royally dressed*
Heore richesse con seye no wiht   *Their; gainsay; person*
265 Of clothes, gurdeles, and other thing,   *girdles (belts)*
Everiche sqyyer thoughte a kyng.   *Every; seemed*
And alle ride of riche aray
Bote Kyng Robert, as I you say.   *Except*
Alle men on him gon pyke,   *look*
270 For he rod al other unlyke.   *rode*
An ape rod of his clothing,   *rode in the same clothing*
In tokne that he was underlyng.   *As a sign he was an underling*

The pope and the emperour also
And other lordes mony mo   *more*
275 Welcomede the angel as for kyng,
And made joye of his comyng.
Theose threo bretheren made cumfort;   *three brothers*
The angel was brother mad bi sort;   *made by necessity*
Wel was the pope and emperour   *Great*
280 That hedden a brother of such honour.   *had*
Forth con sturte Kyng Robert   *leapt*
As fool and mon that nas not fert,   *afraid*
And criyede with ful egre speche   *fierce*
To his bretheren to don him wreche   *brothers revenge him*
285 Of him that hath with queynte gyle   *On him who has with clever guile*
His coroune and lond of Cisyle.   *crown; land*
The pope ne the emperour nouther,   *nor; neither*
The fol ne kneugh not for heor brother.   *fool; knew; their*
Tho was he more fol iholde,   *Therefore; fool considered*
290 More then er a thousend folde;   *before; times*
To cleyme such a bretherhede: *claim; brotherhood*
Hit was holde a foles dede.   *considered; fool's deed*
Kyng Robert bigon to maken care,   *to grieve*
Muche more then he dude are,   *did before*
295 Whon his bretheren nolde him knowe: *When; brothers did not*
"Allas," quath he, "nou am I lowe."   *said*
For he hopede, bi eny thing,   *hoped, somehow*
His bretheren wolde ha mad him kyng;   *brothers; have*
And whon his hope was al ago,   *when; gone*
300 He seide "allas" and "weilawo."   *alas; wellaway*
He seide "allas" that he was bore,   *born*
For he was a mon forlore;
He seide "allas" that he was mad,   *made*
For of his lyf he was al sad.
305 "Allas, allas," was al his song:
His heer he tar, his hondes wrong,   *hair; tore; wrung*
And evere he seide, "Allas, Allas."
And thenne he thoughte on his trespas.
He thoughte on Nabugodonosore,   *Nebuchadnezzar*
310 A noble kyng, was him bifore.   *before him*
In al the world nas his peer,   *was not his equal*
Forte acounte, fer ne neer.   *According to the record, far nor near*
With him was Sire Olyferne,   *Holofernes*
Prince of knihtes stout and steorne.   *bold; stern*
315 Olyferne swor evermor   *swore*
Bi god Nabugodonosor,   *By*
And seide ther nas no god in londe   *was no*
But Nabugodonosor, ich understonde.   *Except; I*
Therfore Nabugodonosor was glad,

320	That he the name of god had,	
	And lovede Olofern the more;	
	And seythe hit greved hem bothe sore.	*later; grieved them; sorely*
	Olofern dyyede in dolour,	*died; sorrow*
	He was slaye in hard schour.	*slain; pain*
325	Nabugodonosor lyvede in desert;	*lived*
	Dorst he noughwher ben apert;	*Dared he nowhere be seen*
	Fyftene yer he livede thare	*there*
	With rootes, gras, and evel fare.	*roots, grass, and poor food*
	And al of mos his clothing was:	*moss*
330	Al com that bi Godes gras:	*by; grace*
	He criyede merci with delful chere,	*cried mercy; sorrowful countenance*
	God him restored, as he was ere.	*before*
	"Nou am I in such caas,	*Now; condition*
	And wel worse then he was.	*much worse*
335	Whon God gaf me such honour,	*When; gave*
	That I was clepet conquerour,	*called*
	In everi lond of Cristendome	
	Of me men speke wel ilome;	*spoke; often*
	And seiden, noughwher was my peer	*said, nowhere; equal (peer)*
340	In al the world, fer no neer.	*far nor near*
	For that name I hedde pride,	*Because of that name (reputation) I had pride*
	As angels that gonne from joye glyde,	*Like angels that from joy fell*
	And in twynklyng of an eighe	*eye*
	God binom heore maystrie.	*took away their power*
345	So hath he myn, for my gult,	*guilt*
	Now am I wel lowe ipult,	*brought down*
	And that is right that I so be.	
	Lord, on Thi fool Thow have pité.	*pity*
	I hedde an errour in myn herte,	*had*
350	And that errour doth me smerte.	*pain*
	Lord, I leeved not on The.	*believed*
	On Thi fol Thou have pité.	
	Holy Writ I hedde in dispyt,	*held in contempt*
	For that is reved my delyt,	*taken away my delight*
355	For that is riht a fool I be,	
	Lord, on Thi fool Thou have pité.	
	Lord I am Thi creature,	
	This wo is riht that I endure,	*woe*
	And wel more, yif hit may be.	*if it*
360	Lord, on Thi fool Thou have pité.	
	Lord, I have igult The sore.	*offended You sorely*
	Merci, Lord, I nul no more;	*will not*
	Evere Thi fol, Lord, wol I be.	*will*
	Lord, on Thi fol Thou have pité.	
365	Blisful Marie, to the I crie,	*Mary; you; cry*
	As thou art ful of cortesye,	*courtesy*

Preye thi Sone, that dyed for me,   *Pray*
On me, His fol, thow have pité.
Blisful Marie, ful of graas,   *grace*
370 To the I knowe my trespas;   *you; acknowledge*
Prey thi Sone, for love of the   *Pray*
On me, His fool, thow have pité."
He seide no more "Allas, Allas!"
But thonked Crist of His gras,   *thanked; grace*
375 And thus he gon himself stille   *be quiet*
And thonked Crist mid good wille.   *with*
Then pope, emperour, and kyng
Fyve wikes made heore dwellyng.   *Five weeks made their abode*
Whon fyve wykes weore agon,   *When five weeks had passed*
380 To heore owne lond heo wolden anon,   *their; wanted to go*
Bothe emperour and the kyng;
Ther was a feir departyng.   *fair*
The angel com to Cisyle,
He and his men, in a while.
385 Whon he com into halle,   *When*
The fool anon he bad forth calle.
He seide: "Fool, art thow kyng?"   *are you*
"Nay, sire," quath he, "withoute lesyng."   *said; lying*
"What artou?" seide the angel.   *are you*
390 "Sire, a fol, that wot I wel,   *know*
And more then fol, yif hit may be;   *if it*
Kep I non other dignité."   *desire*
The angel into chaumbre went,
And after the fol anon he sent.   *at once*
395 He bad his men out of chaumbre gon,   *bade; go*
Ther lafte no mo but he alon   *There were left no more*
And the fol that stod him bi.   *stood; by*
To him he seide: "Thou hast merci!   *forgiveness*
Thenk, thou weore lowe ipult,   *Think; were brought down*
400 And al was for thin owne gult.   *guilt*
A fool thou weore to Hevene kyng,
Therfore thou art an underlyng.   *underling*
God hath forgiven thi mysdede,   *misdeed*
Evere herafter thou him drede!   *dread*
405 I am an angel of renoun,
Isent to kepe thi regioun;   *Sent to protect your region*
More joye me schal falle   *befall*
In hevene among my feren alle   *companions*
In an houre of a day
410 Then in eorthe, I the say,   *earth, I tell you*
In an hundred thousend yeer,
Theigh al the world, fer and neer,   *Though*
Weore myn at my lykyng.   *Were*

I am an angel, thou art kyng!"
415   He went in twynklyng of an eye;
No more of him ther nas seye.   *seen*
Kyng Robert com into halle,
His men he bad anon forth calle,   *bade at once*
And alle weore at his wille,   *were*
420   As to heore lord, as hit was skille.   *their; as it was right*
He lovede God and holi churche,   *Holy Church*
And evere he thoughte wel to worche.   *to do good*
He regned after two yer and more
And lovede God and his lore.   *teaching*
425   The angel gaf him in warnyng   *gave*
Of the tyme of his diying.   *dying*
Whon tyme com to dyye son,   *When; soon*
He let write hit riht anon,   *had it written; immediately*
Hou God myd His muchel miht   *with His great*
430   Made him lowe, as hit was riht.   *just*
This storie he sende everidel   *every bit of it*
To his bretheren, under his seel.   *brothers; seal*
And the tyme, whon he schulde dye   *when; die*
That tyme he diyede as he gon seye.   *died*
435   Al this is writen withouten lyye,   *lies*
At Roome to ben in memorie   *be*
At Seint Petres chirche, I knowe.
And thus is Godes miht isowe,   *disseminated*
That heighe beoth lowe, theigh hit ben ille,   *high; though it be*
440   And lowe heighe, at Godes wille.
Crist, that for us gon dye,   *died*
In His kyneriche let us ben heighe,   *royal lineage; be elevated*
Evermore to ben above,
444   Ther is joye, cumfort and love. Amen.

❧ NOTES TO *ROBERT OF CISYLE*

I have used the following abbreviations in these textual and explanatory notes: **FH**: French and Hale, *Middle English Metrical Romances*; **H**: Horstmann, *Sammlung ae Legenden*; **N**: R. Nuck, *Roberd of Cisyle*; **S**: Simons, "A Byzantine Identity for *Robert of Cisyle*"; **V**: Vernon Manuscript. H and N "modernize" the text with variants from fragmentary manuscripts. V, however, is the most coherent witness; Simeon follows V closely. Therefore, I have based my text on V with some modifications from H, N, and FH. V has Robert as the name of the hero. Other MSS have Roberd; N rhymes with *ferd* (line 282).

1	Formulas such as *princes proude*, *proude in pres*, are common in the poem.
2	I have printed *you* for V *ou*. I have, however, retained most dialectal spellings: e.g., *heo, heore, weore, beo*, for *he, their, were, be*; *uch* for *ech(e)*; *mon, mony* for *man, many*.
3	*Cisyle*: Sicily. The history of Sicily has been turbulent, in part because of its proximity to opportunists from Italy, North Africa, and Spain. It was a perennial site of conflict for the Pope and the Holy Roman Empire. I have not been able to find any historical basis for the brotherhood of Robert, Urban, and Valemounde. There is no evidence for an Emperor Valemounde. Pope Urban IV (1261–64) was deeply involved in Sicilian affairs and there was Saracen involvement in Sicily from the ninth century. However, the familial configuration seems wholly fictional.
13	*nas*: *n* for an initial consonant was a standard form of negation.
15	Hopkins, "Roberd of Cisyle," pp. 194–95, notes that the poem views Robert in isolation; Robert's personal spiritual growth is the focus of the poem, and he performs no knightly deeds, nor is he seen as king.
21	S, pp. 106–07, speculates Valemounde could be a Greek narrator's attempt to pronounce "Bohemund," "a restless and warlike adventurer," and notes his legacy as an enemy of Byzantium and a campaigner against Saracens in Sicily.
29	*Seynt Jones Niht*: Saint John's Night (June 24, the feast of St. John the Baptist).
31	*evensong*: vespers, "usually celebrated shortly before sunset" (OED). The Magnificat (line 35) is a regular part of vespers.
35	See note to lines 40–41.
40–41	These lines are from the Magnificat, Mary's revelation of her divine pregnancy to her sister Elizabeth. The whole passage, now a prayer, is found in Luke 1:46–55:

"He hath put down the mighty from their seat, and hath exalted the humble" (Luke 1:52). V: *exultavit* should be *exaltavit*.

60	It is impossible to say what the "book" is, or if there was one. See Hornstein, "King Robert of Sicily," p. 13, for a discussion of manuscript variations. FH, p. 935, assume the reference is to a written source; Olsen, "Oral Tradition," p. 77, argues "the phrase is a 'tag' line whose only purpose is to provide the poet with a rhyming word and therefore indicates oral transmission."
62, 63	*gan*: "began to" or "did," a common auxiliary of incipient or preterit aspect.
66	S notes that Orthodox theology regards the liturgy as a space out of time, through which angels may come to participate in the service; Sicily's Norman rulers accepted some Greek liturgical practices, as well as other Byzantine customs, despite their devotion to the Latin church (p. 108).
75	*sexteyn*: The sexton is "a church official having the care of the fabric [church building] and its contents" (OED).
79	V: *ffelenye*. V also doubles initial *f* at line 247 (*ffool*) and line 249 (*ffoxes*). I have singled the *f*'s since the usual doubling as a form of capitalization does not apply.
117	*ryght*. Not in V, H, or FH. Emendation based on Harley 525 for meter.
142	For more on the religious origins of Robert's fool status, see Baker ("*Deposuit potentes*," pp. 36–37), and S (pp. 109–10).
154–55	Medieval fools were sometimes shaved, as were monastics and penitents, to mark their special status. Diseases, like madness, were perceived as divine punishment for sin; some medieval medical texts recommended shaving a madman's head as part of treatment. See Harper, *Insanity, Individuals, and Society*.
157	The ape also represents madmen, sinners, penitents, and the sin of pride. See Hopkins, "Roberd of Cisyle," p. 188, and Hornstein, "King Robert of Sicily," p. 19.
166	An assayer could be either a server (waiter) or a taster, for safety's sake (OED).
195	FH emend V *he* to *him*, but, following H, N, I do not see the necessity.
232	Holy Thursday, the day commemorating Jesus' Last Supper with the apostles.
255	V: *Al whit atyr was*; FH, following H: *Al was whit, atyr*.
281	V: *com*, but there is merit in FH: *con*. FH, following V, have Robert as the last word in the line and the rhyme word in line 282 is *fert* (afraid).
315–16	King Nebuchadnezzar and General Holofernes appear in the apocryphal Book of Judith, when the king sends the general to put down the Jewish defense of Jerusalem from Bethulia. Judith entices and beheads Holofernes; after he has blasphemously called the king a god (line 316), Holofernes' fall (line 323) is thus apt. See "The Story of Judith," in *Heroic Women from the Old Testament in Middle English Verse*, ed. Russell A. Peck (Kalamazoo, MI: Medieval Institute Publications, 1991), and Penelope Doob, *Nebuchadnezzar's Children: Conventions of Madness in*

Middle English Literature (New Haven, CT: Yale University Press, 1974). For analysis of the Nebuchadnezzar episode, see Hopkins, "Roberd of Cisyle," pp. 189–92.

325   Nebuchadnezzar's fifteen years in the desert living on roots, grass, and poor food (lines 327–28) derives particularly from Daniel 4:22. For a detailed discussion of that passage in Middle English literature, see Russell A. Peck, "John Gower and the Book of Daniel," in *John Gower: Recent Readings*, ed. R. F. Yeager (Kalamazoo, MI: Medieval Institute Publications, 1989), pp. 159–87. Peck does not mention *Robert of Cisyle*.

342   *As*. V: *And*, followed by FH. H's emendation.

344   FH states "the construction is faulty, the sense clear" in lines 341–44, and N reads "*As in*" at line 343 (p. 935); Olsen argues FH and N presuppose a written source, and the erratic grammar suggests oral transmission ("Oral Tradition," pp. 73–74).

352   *On*. Trinity and Harley 1701 read: *Lord on*, followed by H and FH. The anaphora is compelling but not necessary.

358   *endure*. V: *dure*, followed by H and FH.

388   *"withoute lesyng."* H leaves out quotation marks.

✣✣ INTRODUCTION TO *SIR AMADACE*

The complexity of the apparently simple *Sir Amadace* lies in the ambiguity of its ideal. The poem uses much of the idealistic paraphernalia of conventional romance in the exposition of an ideal that sometimes seems merely materialistic. Is *Sir Amadace* a story of generosity put to the test and finally vindicated? Or is it just a story of wealth lost and regained? Traditionally, the values of the romance hero are vindicated by the complicit universe in which he lives. Certainly Sir Amadace, despite his tribulations, is, like more obviously altruistic romance heroes, in the right world at the right time. The narrator seems to imply that Amadace's predicament is the result of excessive, but basically admirable, liberality; he may be foolish, but he is not evil, and therefore deserves the restoration of his wealth. It is hard to ignore, however, the pervasively materialistic context in which the "ideal" is represented. This discontinuity between the vision of the narrator and the tendency of the narrative makes a slight, amusing story problematic and fascinating.

The version of *Sir Amadace* presented here is from the Ireland Manuscript, but it differs little from the version in the Advocates Manuscript. Although neither version seems derived from the other or from an identifiable common source, the ambiguities of idealism and materialism are prominent in both. Despite uncertainty about what its moral "lesson" is, the poem is a good specimen of whatever it is. The twelve-line stanza rhymed *aabccbddbeeb* in tetrameters except for trimeters in the B lines, provides a compact structural unit that is generally executed successfully. The movement is lively and the story, no matter what it means or implies, is engaging. The romance is not even bourgeois; it often seems the most lower class of romances, celebrating money and its associated power from a vantage point near the bottom of the social scale. It is popular not aristocratic, indeed, a view of the world, or the world of romance, from the perspective of the underclasses who mistake the bourgeois for the noble. And perhaps that is why moral idealism and material well-being become so intriguingly intertwined. All of the ingredients of romance are there, and all of the ingredients of didactic narrative, as well as a fair helping of folklore. Yet, largely because of the ambiguity of its ideal, *Sir Amadace* remains a good story that defies literary taxonomy.

Both versions (those in the Ireland and the Advocates Manuscripts) are acephalous. We enter the story when it is already clear that something has gone seriously wrong with Amadace's finances. His expenses exceed his income, and he is down to his last forty pounds. He reminds us of other admirable "spendthrift knights" like Sir Launfal and Sir Cleges. However, Launfal's decline in wealth is largely attributable to the malice of Guenevere and Cleges' extravagance is more fully and sympathetically described. With Amadace, perhaps because the poem is acephalous, his steward, a pragmatic rather than an evil one in this poem, gives him some straight talk:

"Sir, ye awe wele more	*steward; owe much more*
Thenne ye may of your londus rere	*Than; lands collect*
In faythe this sevyn yere.	*seven years*
Quoso may best, furste ye mun pray,	*Whoever best; must ask*
Abyde yo till anothir day.	*Endure you*
And parte your cowrte in sere;	*divide your court in parts*
And putte away full mony of your men;	*many*
And hald butte on, quere ye hald ten,	*keep but one, where you kept*
Thaghe thay be nevyr so dere."	*Though; never*

(lines 4–12)

Whether the cause is liberality or prodigality, Amadace is facing a version of "romance adversity." If he is guilty it seems likely that his failure is foolishness rather than self-indulgence. He honorably refuses to force payment from his debtors but foolishly wants to leave with a last flourish:

"Yette wille I furst, or I fare,	*first, before I travel*
Be wele more riall then I was are,	*royal; before*
Therfore ordan thu schall,	*decree you*
For I wulle gif full ryche giftus	*will give; gifts*
Bothe to squiers and to knyghtis;	*squires*
To pore men dele a dole.	*give alms*

(lines 37–42)

He departs, like Sir Orfeo, not in order to do something specific, to take on some well-defined quest, but in reaction to the way things are at his court. Unlike Orfeo, he is not motivated by the desperation of the human agony of lost love, but by the need to avoid his creditors until his income catches up with his expenses. He is buying time; presumably he will not be able to get further into debt in the woods; if he has a plan it is not related to anything but regaining financial solvency.

When he comes upon the stinking chapel (the elaborate insistence on the stench is one of the things that keeps his nobility in perspective), with the weeping wife and unburied husband, he has a folkloric opportunity. The dead man cannot be buried because of his debts; this has an ominous ring to it. Why the merchant, who is the creditor, has such power over the body and soul of the knight is not made clear in the story, but the problem is common in folklore. Amadace's immediate reaction is identification with the victim — for good reason. Despite the "self-interest," his expenditure of his last forty pounds, thirty for the creditor and ten for burial and memorials, suggests that his own difficulties are the result of instinctive generosity rather than profligacy. The problem is that the situation is framed in such wholly economic terms that it is difficult to focus on the spiritual dimensions that the poem's didactic intentions seem to call for.

Pointlessly proceeding into the woods, penniless, Amadace is visited by a "white knight." Although we are not told explicitly, this knight seems to be a manifestation of the knight he has buried and becomes a guide. The white knight's advice is curious. He comforts Amadace and urges him to seek out the marriageable daughter of the king. Why Amadace is wandering, for what specific purpose, is not clear, nor is the motive of the mysterious white knight. Unlike its analogues, this poem does not have Amadace set off on a quest for a specific rich maiden. It is also clear that his spiritual guide, however helpful, is duplicitous. He recommends that Amadace present himself as the victim of a shipwreck to explain his lack of companions; there is enough of a real wreck nearby, apparently magically provided, for Amadace to equip himself plausibly. The white knight, however, is not simply a "romance engineer," a figure sent to lead the hero in a direction that will prove successful and establish the hero's essential harmony with the world he lives in. The white knight is oddly commercial even in referring to God when he counsels Amadace that Amadace's situation is the way of the world, but that God will set things right and, even more strongly, when he insists on half of whatever Amadace gets from the mercenary quest he has set him on.

Warmly received at court, Amadace wins a series of tournaments and gives half of the proceeds to the king, "nobly" reserving half for the white knight whom he knows he owes. Amadace also wins the love of the king's daughter, and has a child, wherein lies the problem when the white knight returns to collect his "half." Amadace, with his wife's devoted compliance, is willing to have her and their child riven in half in order to keep his word to the white knight. Fortunately, if predictably, the white knight relents — he is after all "a good guy" and in fact the person whose burial Amadace arranged — and praises the wife for her loyalty. The white knight then departs, Amadace pays off his debts, the king conveniently dies, and Amadace inherits the kingdom.

Although the elements and impulse of romance are present, there is an insistently commercial quality about the story of Amadace that limits the idealism and may finally compromise his eventual success. As a romance, *Sir Amadace* is based on the folk motif of "the grateful dead" and its hero's behavior is shaped accordingly. Like countless knights of romance he is beset by misfortune, undertakes a vague quest, behaves generously to the unburied knight, wins jousts, overcomes adversity with the magical help of the white knight, and finds a rich and happy ending. The form fits and yet the poem remains oddly ambiguous as romance, though fascinating as narrative.

This narrator implies that this is all to be taken as the story of the reward for Amadace's original liberality: his generosity got him into difficulties but God restores him because his insolvency was the result of noble impulses. But these hints do not seem to be fully developed or realized in the plot. As a result, *Sir Amadace* seems to be a "commercial romance." The structural elements of traditional romance are present, but there is a peculiar reduction of ideals to wealth. It is not simply that Amadace is too middle class to be a romance hero. Long before, *Havelok* presented us with a romance hero not even middle but lower class. However, the terms of Havelok's situation are different. Havelok's means, and much of his heroism, are lower class, not even bourgeois, while his ideals are transcendent. Amadace is further up the social scale, but his context and motives, despite the shape of romance, remain material and mercantile. There are many noble and magical ornaments, but this finally is a story of a knight who gets out of debt.

Amadace's original plight is material, his succor of the unburied knight is material, the white knight's assistance to him is material, his redemption is material (paying off his debts), and his ultimate happiness is material. Yet the narrator seems to hope that we will somehow make something more of all this. This is not to say that it is a poorly made or unworthy poem, but it does take the form and matter of folklore and romance and turn them not to the celebration of moral idealism but to the vindication of material well-being. Doubtless the poem is also didactic, but its lesson may be more commercial than spiritual and therein lies its special fascination.

Select Bibliography

Manuscripts

Advocates 19.3.1 (formerly Jac V.7.27), at the National Library of Scotland, Edinburgh. Fols. 68r–84r. [1475–1500. 778 lines.]

Ireland Blackburn, at Robert H. Taylor Collection, Princeton University Libraries (Taylor MS. 9). Fols. 16r–34v. [1450–60. 852 lines.]

Previous Editions

Brookhouse, Christopher, ed. *Sir Amadace and The Avowing of Arthur: Two Romances from the Ireland MS.* Anglistica 15. Copenhagen: Rosenkilde and Bagger, 1968. [Ireland MS.]

Mills, Maldwyn. *Six Middle English Romances.* Totowa, NJ: Rowman and Littlefield, 1973. Pp. 169–92.

Robson, John, ed. *Three Early English Metrical Romances.* Camden Society 18. London: John Bowyer Nichols and Son, 1842. Pp. 27–56. [Ireland MS.]

Weber, Henry, ed. *Metrical Romances of the Thirteenth, Fourteenth, and Fifteenth Centuries.* 3 vols. Edinburgh: George Ramsay and Company, 1810. Vol. 3. Pp. 241–75. [Advocates MS.]

Criticism

Foster, Edward E. "Simplicity, Complexity, and Morality in Four Medieval Romances." *Chaucer Review* 31 (1997), 407–19.

Harkins, Patricia. "The Speaking Dead in Sir Amadace and the White Knight." *Journal of the Fantastic in the Arts* 3.3 (1994), 62–71.

Kane, George. *Middle English Literature: A Critical Study of the Romances, the Religious Lyrics, and Piers Plowman.* New York: Barnes and Noble, 1951.

Loomis, Laura Hibbard. *Medieval Romance in England: A Study of the Sources and Analogues of the Noncyclic Metrical Romances.* Second ed. New York: Burt Franklin, 1960.

Putter, Ad. "Gifts and Commodities in *Sir Amadace*." *Review of English Studies* 51 (2000), 371–94.

Williams, Elizabeth. "Sir Amadace and the Undisenchanted Bride: The Relation of the Middle English Romance to the Folktale Tradition of 'The Grateful Dead.'" *Tradition and Transformation in Medieval Romance.* Ed. Rosalind Field. Cambridge: Brewer, 1999. Pp. 57–70.

SIR AMADACE

	Thenne the knyght and the stuard fre,	*steward noble*
	Thay casten there houe hit best myghte be	*calculated; how*
	Bothe be ferre and nere.	*by far and near*
	The stuard sayd, "Sir, ye awe wele more	*steward; owe much more*
5	Thenne ye may of your londus rere	*Than; lands collect*
	In faythe this sevyn yere.	*seven years*
	Quoso may best, furste ye mun pray,	*Whoever best; must ask*
	Abyde yo till anothir day.	*Endure you*
	And parte your cowrte in sere;	*divide your court in parts*
10	And putte away full mony of your men;	*many*
	And hald butte on, quere ye hald ten,	*keep but one, where you kept*
	Thaghe thay be nevyr so dere."	*Though; never*
	Thenne Sir Amadace sayd, "I myghte lung spare	*long economize*
	Or all these godus qwitte ware,	*Before all this money were paid*
15	And have noghte to spend;	*nothing*
	Sithun duell here, quere I was borne,	*Afterwards dwell; where*
	Bothe in hething and in scorne —	*contempt*
	And I am so wele kennit.	*known*
	And men full fast wold ware me,	*very quickly would be wary of me*
20	That of thayre godus hade bynne so fre,	*goods; generous*
	That I have hade in honde.	*had in hand*
	Or I schuld hold men in awe or threte,	*dread; threat*
	That thay myghte noghte hor awne gud gete —	*their own goods*
	Thenne made I a full fowle ende.	*completely disgraceful*
25	"Butte anothir rede I wulle me toe,	*counsel; will; take*
	Wurche anothir way then soe,	*Work; than so*
	Bettur sayd soro thenne sene.	*Better said sorrow be than seen*
	Butte, gode stuard, as thu art me lefe,	*to me dear*
	Lette nevyr mon wete my grete mischefe,	*know; distress*
30	Butte hele hit us betwene.	*hold (keep it a secret)*
	For sevyn yere wedsette my lond	*seven; put as a pledge*
	To the godus that I am awand	*Until the goods; owing*
	Be quytte holly bidene.	*paid back wholly at once*
	For oute of the cuntray I wille weynde,	*go*

35 Quil I have gold, silvyr to spende,	*Until*
And be owte of dette full clene.	
"Yette wille I furst, or I fare,	*first, before I travel*
Be wele more riall then I was are,	*royal; before*
Therfore ordan thu schall,	*decree you*
40 For I wulle gif full ryche giftus	*will give; gifts*
Bothe to squiers and to knyghtis;	*squires*
To pore men dele a dole.	*give alms*
Suche men myghte wete that I were wo,	*know; in difficulty (woe)*
That full fayn wold hit were such toe,	*would very much like; so happened*
45 That myghte notte bete my bale.	*help my trouble*
So curtase a mon was nevyr non borne	*courteous; never none born*
That schuld scape withoute a scorne	*escape*
Be iche mon had told his tale."	*If each man had his story told*
Thanne Sir Amadase, as I yo say,	
50 Hase ordanut him opon a day	*prepared*
Of the cuntray in a stowunde.	*To leave; moment*
Yette he gafe ful riche giftus,	*Beforehand*
Bothe to squiers and to knyghtis,	*squires*
Stedus, haukes, and howundes.	*Horses, hawks; hounds*
55 Sethun afturward, as I yo say,	*Then*
Hase ordanut him opon a day,	*prepared*
And furthe thenne conne he founde.	*forth; he set out*
Be that he toke his leve to wynde.	*leave to travel*
He lafte no more in his cofurs to spende,	*left; coffers*
60 But evyn forty powunde.	*only; pounds*
Thenne Sir Amadace, as I yo say,	
Rode furthe opon his way,	*forth*
Als fast as evyr he myghte.	*As; ever*
Throowte a forest, by one cité,	*Beyond; city*
65 Ther stode a chapell of stone and tre,	*stood; wood*
And therinne se he a lighte.	*saw*
Commawundut his knave for to fare,	*Commanded; young servant; go*
To wete quat lighte that were thare —	*find out what*
"And tithing bring me ryghte."	*news; directly*
70 The knave did as his maister him bade,	*young servant*
Butte suche a stinke in the chapell he hade,	*experienced*
That dwelle ther he ne myghte.	*remain*
He stopput his nase with his hude;	*stopped; nose; hood*
Nerre the chapell dur he yode,	*Nearer; door; made his way*
75 Anturs for to lere.	*Adventures; learn*
And as he loket in atte the glasse,	*looked in at the window*
To wete quat mervail that ther wasse,	*find out what marvel*

So see he stonde a bere.   *stood a bier*
Candils ther were brennyng toe,   *burning two*
80   A woman sittyng, and no moe.   *more*
Lord! carefull wasse hur chere.   *sorrowful was her expression*
Tithinges there conne he non frayn,   *News; he did not try to ask*
Butte to his lord he wente agayn,
Told him quat he see thare.   *what*

85   And sayd, "Sir, atte yondur chapell have I bene,
A selcothe sighte ther have I sene,   *strange*
My herte is hevy as lede.   *heavy as lead*
Ther stondus a bere and canduls toe;   *stands a bier; two*
Ther sittus a woman, and no moe.   *sits; more*
90   Lord! carefull is hur rede.   *sorrowful is her countenance*
Suche a stinke as I had thare,
Sertis thenne had I nevyr are   *Certainly; before*
Noquere in no stid.   *Nowhere; place*
For this palfray that I on ryde,   *horse (for riding)*
95   Ther myghte I no lengur abide;   *longer remain*
I traue I have keghte my dede."   *believe; incurred my death*

Thenne Sir Amadace commawundut his squier to fare,   *commanded; go*
To witte quat woman that there ware,   *find out what*
"And tithinges bring thu me."   *news*
100   As he loket in atte the walle,   *looked*
As the knave sayd, he fund withalle,   *young man; found withal*
Him thoghte hit grete peté.   *pity*
Butte in his nace smote such a smell,   *But; nose struck*
That there myghte he no lengur duelle,   *remain*
105   But sone agayn gose he.   *goes*
He sayd, "Gud Lord, nowe with your leve,   *permission*
I pray yo take hit noghte on greve,
For ye may notte wete for me."   *nothing learn*

He sayd, "Sir, ther stondus a bere, and candils toe,   *stands a bier; two*
110   A woman sittyng, and no moe.   *more*
Lord! carefull is hur chere.   *sorrowful; expression*
Sore ho sikes and hondus wringus,   *Sorely she sighs; hands wrings*
And evyr ho crius on hevyn kynges,   *always she cries*
How lung ho schall be thare.   *long she*
115   Ho says, Dere God, quat may that be,   *She; what*
The grete soro that ho opon him se,   *sorrow; she*
Stingcand opon his bere,   *Rotting*
Ho says, ho will notte leve him allone   *She; not leave*
Till ho fall dede downe to the stone,   *she*
120   For his life was hur full dere."   *(to) her; very dear*

	Thenne Sir Amadace smote his palfray with his spur,	*struck; horse; his*
	And rode unto the chapell dur;	*door*
	And hastele doune he lighte.	*hastily; alit*
	As his menne sayd, so con him thinke	*man; it seemed to him*
125	That he nevyr are hade such a stynke,	*before*
	And inne thenne wente that knyghte.	
	He sayd, "Dame, God rest with the,"	
	Ho sayd, "Sir, welcum most ye be."	*She*
	And salit him anon ryghte.	*greeted; directly*
130	He sayd, "Dame, quy sittus thu here	*why; sit*
	Kepand this dede cors opon this bere,	*Watching ever; corpse*
	Thus onyli upon a nyghte?"	*alone*
	Ho sayd, "Sir, nedelonges most I sitte him by,	*necessarily must*
	Hifath, ther will him non mon butte I,	*In faith; no one*
135	For he wasse my wedutte fere."	*wedded companion*
	Thenne Sir Amadace sayd, "Me likes full ill,	
	Ye ar bothe in plyit to spille,	*danger of destruction*
	He lise so lung on bere.	*lies; long; bier*
	Quat a mon in his lyve wasse he?"	*What; life*
140	"Sir, a marchand of this cité,	*merchant*
	Hade riche rentus to rere.	*rents; collect*
	And eviryche yere thre hundrythe powndee	*every; hundred pounds*
	Of redy monay and of rowunde,	*round (i.e., coins)*
	And for dette yette lise he here."	*debt; lies*
145	Thenne Sir Amadace sayd, "For the Rode,	*By the Cross*
	On quat maner spendutte he his gud	*In what; spent; substance*
	That thusgate is away?"	*thus*
	"Sir, on gentilmen and officers,	
	On grete lordus, that was his perus,	*lords; peers*
150	Wold giffe hom giftus gay.	*them gifts*
	Riche festus wold he make,	*feasts*
	And pore men, for Goddus sake,	
	He fed hom evyriche day.	*them every*
	Quil he hade any gud to take,	*While; possessions*
155	He wernut no mon, for Goddus sake,	*refused*
	That wolnotte onus say nay.	*would not once say no*
	"Yette he didde as a fole.	*behaved; fool*
	He cladde mo men agaynus a yole	*clothed more; Christmas season*
	Thenne did a nobull knyghte:	*Than*
160	For his mete he wold not spare;	*food*
	Burdes in the halle were nevyr bare,	*Boards (tables)*
	With clothes richeli dighte.	*prepared*
	Giffe I sayd he did noghte wele,	*If*
	He sayd, God send hit everyche dele,	

165 And sette my wurdus atte lighte. *dismissed my words lightly*
Bi thenne he toke so mycul opon his name, *much*
That I dar notte telle yo, lord, for schame
The godus now that he aghte. *goods; owed*

"And thenne come dethe, wo hym be,
170 And partutt my lord and me, *parted*
Lafte me in all the care.
Quen my neghteburs herd telle that he seke lay, *When; neighbors*
Thay come to me, as thay best may,
Thair gud aschet thai thare. *goods asked for*
175 All that evyr was his and myne,
Hors and naute, shepe and squwyne, *Horses; cattle; sheep; swine*
Away thay drafe and bare. *drove; bore*
My dowary to my lyve I sold, *dowry*
And all the peneys to hom told. *pennies; them counted out*
180 Lord! Yette aghte he wele mare. *owed; more*

"Quen I hade quytte all that I myghte gete, *When; paid back*
Yette aghte he thritté powunde bi grete, *owed; on demand*
Holly till a stydde; *Wholly at a time*
Till a marchand of this cité, *merchant*
185 Was fer oute in anothir cuntré,
Come home quen he was dede. *when*
And quenne he herd telle of my febull fare, *when; poor condition*
He come to me as breme as bare, *as ferociously as a boar*
This corse the erthe forbede, *corpse; forbade*
190 And sayd, howundus schuld his bodi to draw, *hounds should; tear apart*
Then on the fild his bonus tognaue. *field; bones gnaw on*
Thus carefull is my rede. *sorrowful; countenance*

"And this sixtene weke I have setyn here, *sat*
Kepand this dede cors opon this bere, *Watching over; dead corpse; bier*
195 With candils brennand bryghte. *burning*
And so schall I evyrmore do,
Till dethe cum and take me to,
Bi Mary, most of myghte!"
Thenne Sir Amadace franut hur the marchandes name *asked her; merchant's*
200 That hade done hur all that schame.
Ho told him anon ryghte. *She; directly*
He sayd, "God that is bote of all bale, *help; trouble*
Dame, cumford the, and so He schale; *comfort you*
And, Dame, have thu gud nyghte."

A Fitte
205 Thenne Sir Amadace on his palfray lepe; *leapt*
Unnethe he myghte forgoe to wepe, *Scarcely he can*

	For his dedus him sore forthoghte;	*deeds; regretted*
	Sayd, "Yondur mon that lise yondur chapell withinne,	*man; lies*
	He myghte full wele be of my kynne,	
210	For ryghte so have I wroghte."	*just so; wrought*
	Thenne he told his sometour quat the marchand heght,[1]	
	And sayd, "I will sowpe with him tonyghte,	*eat*
	Be God that me dere boghte!	*By; dearly bought (redeemed)*
	Go, loke thu dighte oure soper syne,	*prepare; then*
215	Gode ryall metis and fyne,	*Good royal meats*
	And spicis thenne spare thu noghte."	*spices*

	And sone quen the sometour herd,	*soon when; pack-horse driver*
	To the marchandus howse he ferd,	*merchant's; went*
	And ordanut for that knyghte.	*prepared*
220	Thenne Sir Amadace come riding thoe,	*at that time*
	But in his hert was him full woe,	
	And hasteli dowun he lighte.	*hastily down he dismounted*
	Sithun intylle a chambur the knyghte yede,	*Then into; went*
	And kest opon him othir wede,	*put on; clothes*
225	With torches brennyng bryghte.	*burning*
	He cummawundutte his squier for to goe,	*commanded*
	To pray the marchand and his wife allsoe	
	To soupe with him that nyghte.	*eat*

	Thenne the squier weyndut upon his way,	*went*
230	And to the marchand conne he say;	*began*
	His ernde told he thenne.	*message*
	He squere, "Be Jhesu, Mare sone,	*swore By Jesus, Mary's son*
	That Lordus will hit schall be done,	*Lord's; it*
	Of cumford was that man."	*comfort*
235	Thenne thayre soper was nere dighte;	*supper; almost prepared*
	Burdes were hovyn hee on lighte;	*Boards; placed high*
	The marchand the dees began.	*merchant; high table*
	Sir Amadace sate, and made gud chere,	
	Butte on the dede cors that lay on bere	
240	Ful mycull his thoghte was on.	*much*

	Sir Amadace sayd, "Tonyghte as I come bi the strete,	
	I see a sighte I thenke on yete,	*yet*
	That sittus me nowe full sore.	*grieves*
	In a chapell beside a way	
245	A dede cors opon a bere lay,	
	A womon all mysfare."	*come to grief*
	"Ye," the marchand sayd "God gif him a sore grace,	

Then he told his pack-horse driver what the merchant promised

And all suche waisters as he wasse,   *wasters (spendthrifts)*
For he sittus me nowe sare;   *grieves*
250   For he lise there with my thritti powunde   *lies; thirty pounds*
Of redy monay and of rowunde,   *round (i.e., coins)*
Of hitte gete I nevyr more."

Thenne Sir Amadace sayd, "Take the till a bettur rede,   *better advice*
Thenke that Gode forgave His dede.   *death*
255   Grete merit thu may have.
Thenke how God ordant for the   *ordained*
Bettur grace then evyr had He.
Lette the cors go inne his grave."   *corpse*
Thenne he squere, "Be Jhesu, Mare sun,   *swore*
260   That body schall nevyr in the erthe come
My silvyr tille that I have;   *silver until*
Till ho be ded as wele as he,   *Until she*
That howundus schall, that I may se,   *hounds*
On filde thayre bonus tognaue."   *field their bones gnaw*

265   Quen Sir Amadace herd that he hade squorne,   *When; sworn*
He cald his stuard him beforne,   *called*
Of kyndenesse that knyghte con kithe,   *did show*
And bede, "Go foche me thritti powunde   *bade; fetch; thirty pounds*
Of redy monay and of rowunde,   *Of cash (spendable money); round (i.e., coins)*
270   Hastely and belyve."   *hastily; quickly*
The stuard thoghte hit was agaynus skille,   *contrary to reason*
Butte he most nede do his maistur wille —
Now listun and ye may lithe.   *hear*
Ther Sir Amadace payd him thritti powund of monay fyne.   *finally*
275   And thenne Sir Amadace asket to wyne,   *asked*
And prayd the marchand be blythe.   *merchant; happy*

Then Sir Amadace asket, "Awe he the any mare?"   *asked; Owed*
"Nay, Sir," he sayd, "wele most ye fare.
For thus muche he me aghte."   *owed*
280   Thenne Sir Amadace sayd, "As furthe as ten pounde will take   *far; accomplish*
I schall lette do for his sake,
Querthroghe he have his righte.   *Whereby; rites*
I schall for him gere rede and singe,   *arrange readings and singing*
Bringe his bodi to Cristun berunge,   *Christian burial*
285   That schall thu see wythe sighte.
Go pray all the religius of this cité   *religious*
Tomorne that thay wold dyne with me,
And loke thayre mete be dyghte."   *And see their food be prepared*

Howe erly quen day con spring,   *when; began*
290   Then holli all the bellus con ring   *bells; began*

	That in the cité was.	*everyone*
	Religius men evrichon	
	Toward this dede cors are thay gone	
	With mony a riche burias.	*many a rich burgess*
295	Thritty prustus that day con sing,	*Thirty priests; began*
	And thenne Sir Amadace offurt a ring	*offered*
	Atte evyriche mas.	*every Mass*
	Quen the servise was all done,	*When*
	He prayd hom to ete with him atte none,	*prayed them to eat; at once*
300	Holli more and lasse.	*Wholly*
	Thenne the marchand wente tille one pillere;	*merchant; to; pillar*
	Mony a mon droghe him nere	*drew near him*
	To wete quat he wold say.	*know what*
	He sayd, "Sirs, there hase byn here	
305	A ded cors opon a bere —	*corpse; bier*
	Ye wotte querfore hit lay.	*know; why*
	And hase comun a full riall knyghte,	*has come; royal*
	Of all the godes the cors me heghte	*goods; corpse owed me*
	Hase made me redi pay.	*has*
310	Unto his cofurs he hase sente,	*his coffers*
	And gevyn ten powunde to his termente,	*given; interment*
	Wythe riche ringus today.	*costly rings*
	"Hit is on his nome that I say,	*at his behest*
	He prays yo holly to mete today,	*wholly; dinner*
315	All that ther bene here."	
	Thay did as the marchand bade;	
	Mete and drinke ynughe thay hade,	*enough*
	With licius drinke and clere.	*delicious; sparkling*
	And Sir Amadace wold noghte sitte downe,	
320	Butte to serve the pore folke he was full bowne,	*very ready*
	For thay lay his hert nere.	
	And quen thay hade etun withinne that halle,	*when; eaten*
	Thenne Sir Amadace toke leve atte all,	*leave of all*
	Unsemand with full glad chere.	*Pretending*
325	Quen Sir Amadace hade etun,	*When; eaten*
	To sadull his horse was noghte forgetun,	*saddle; forgotten*
	Thay broghte hym his palfray.	
	Thenne his sometour mon before was dyghte,	*pack-horse driver; prepared*
	Ther as that lord schuld leng all nyghte	*As if; stay*
330	And hade nothing to pay.	
	Quat wundur were hit thaghe him were wo	*What wonder; though*
	Quen all his godus were spendutte him fro,	*When; goods; spent*
	The sothe gif I schuld say?	*truth if*
	Thenne Sir Amadace kidde he was gentilman bornne,	*revealed*

335	He come the grattust maystur beforne,	*went to the greatest lord there*
	Tok leve, and wente his way.	*Took leave*
	Quen he was gone on this kin wise,	*kind of way*
	Thenne iche mon sayd thayre devise,	*opinion*
	Quen he wasse passutte the gate.	*When; passed*
340	Sum sayd, "This gud full lighteli he wan,	*wealth; lightly; acquired*
	That thusgate spendutte hit on this man,	*thus spent*
	So lightely lete hit scape."	*easily*
	Sum sayd, "In gud tyme were he borne	
	That hade a peny him biforne,"	*penny (bit of money)*
345	That knew full litull his state.	*Who; situation*
	Lo, how thay demun the gentill knyghte,	*judged*
	Quen he hade spendut all that he myghte.	*When; spent*
	Butte the trauthe full litull thay wote.	*truth; knew*
	Quen he come sex mile the cité fro,	*When*
350	A crosse partut the way atoe.	*cross parted; in two*
	Thenne speke Sir Amadace:	
	To his stuard he sayd full rathe,	*quickly*
	His sometour and his palfray mon bothe,	*pack-horse driver; groom*
	And all ther evyr was,	
355	Sayd, "Gode sirs, take noghte on greve,	*be not sad*
	For ye most noue take your leve,	*now; leave*
	For youreselvun knauyn the cace;	*yourselves know; case*
	For I may lede no mon in londe,	
	Butte I hade gold and silvyr to spend,	
360	Nevyr no quere in no place."	*where*
	Now the hardust hertut men that there ware,	*hardest hearted*
	For to wepe thai myght notte spare	
	Quen thay herd him say so.	*When*
	He sayd, "Gode sirs, have ye no care,	*sorrow*
365	For ye mone have maysturs evyrqware,	*will have masters*
	As wele wurthi ye ar soe.	*As well worthy as you are*
	Yette God may me sende of his sele,	*largesse*
	That I may kevyr of this full wele,	*recover*
	And cum owte of this wo.	
370	A mery mon yette may ye se me,	*man*
	And be full dere welcum to me,	
	Bothe ye and mony moe."	
	Sir Amadas seyd in that stonde:	*time*
	"Tho warst hors is worthe ten pownde	*worst*
375	Of hom all that here gon.	*them; go*
	Sqwyar, yomon, and knave,	*Squire, yeoman; young man*
	Ylke mon his owne schall have	*Each man*

That he syttes apon.
Sadyll, brydyll, and oder geyre,   *other equipment*
380   Fowre so gud thoffe hit were,
I woch hit save bi Sen Jon.[2]
God mey make yo full gud men.
Chryst of hevon y yo beken!"   *heaven; bid*
Thei weped and partyd ylke on.   *wept; parted each one*

385   Quen all his men was partutte him fro,   *parted*
The knyghte lafte still in all the woe,   *remained*
Bi himselvun allone.   *By himself alone*
Throghe the forest his way lay righte;   *Through*
Of his palfray doune he lighte,   *dismounted*
390   Mournand and made grete mone.   *Mourning; moan*
Quen he thoghte on his londus brode,   *lands broad*
His castels hee, his townus made,   *high; well-constructed*
That were away evyrichon,
That he had sette, and layd to wedde,   *set, and put in mortgage*
395   And was owte of the cuntray for povrté fledde.   *out; poverty*
Thenne the knyghte wexe will of wone.   *grew uncertain of expectation*

Thenne bespeke Sir Amadace,
"A mon that litul gode hase,   *wealth has*
Men sittus ryghte noghte him bye;   *set*
400   For I hade thre hundrythe powunde of rente,
I spendut two in that entente.   *spent; for that purpose*
Of such forloke was I.   *foresight*
Evyr quyll I suche housold hold,   *Always while*
For a grete lord was I tellut,   *reputed*
405   Much holdun uppe thareby.   *Much held up (admired)*
Nowe may wise men sitte atte home,
Quen folus may walke full wille of wone,[3]
And, Christ wotte, so may hi."   *knows; they*

He sayd, "Jhesu, as Thu deet on the Rode,   *died on the Cross*
410   And for me sched Thi precius blode,   *shed*
And all this world Thu wanne;   *won (redeemed)*
Thu lette me nevyr come in that syghte,
Ther I have bene knauen for a knyghte,   *Where; known*
Butte if I may avoue hit thanne.   *Until I may declare it*
415   And gif me grace to somun all tho   *summon; those*
That wilsumly are wente me fro,   *willfully; gone from me*
And all that me gode ons hase done;   *once have done me good*

---

²   *Though it were four times as good (as it is), / I guarantee it by Saint John*

³   *When fools may walk wholly bewildered (homeless)*

Or ellus, Lord, I aske The rede,   *else; help*
Hastely that I were dede,   *dead*
420 Lord, wele were me thanne.   *then*

"For all for wonting of my witte,   *deficiency; wit*
Fowle of the lond am I putte,   *Disgraced in the land I am set*
Of my frindes I have made foes;
For kyndenes of my gud wille,
425 I am in poynte myselfe to spille."   *at the point of being destroyed*
Thus flote Syr Amadace.   *drifted (in mind)*
He say, "Jhesu, as Thu deut on tre,   *died on the tree (cross)*
Summe of Thi sokur and Thu me,   *Some; succor*
Spedely in this place,   *Quickly*
430 For summe of Thi sokur and Thu me send,   *some; succor if*
And yette I schuld ful gladely spende
On all that mestur hase."   *need have*

Now thro the forest as he ferd,   *made his way*
He wende that no mon hade him herd,   *thought; heard*
435 For he seghe no mon in sighte.   *saw*
So come a mon ryding him bye,
And speke on him fulle hastely,
Therof he was afryghte.
Milke quyte was his stede,   *white*
440 And so was all his othir wede —   *clothes*
Hade contiens of a knyghte.   *bearing*
Now thoghe Sir Amadace wasse in mournyng broghte,   *though*
His curtasé forgete he noghte,   *courtesy forgot*
He saylut him anon ryghte.   *saluted; directly*

445 Quod the quite knyghte, "Quat mon is this,   *Said; white; What*
That all this mowrnyng makes thus   *mourning*
With so simpull chere?"   *demeanor*
Thenne Syr Amadace say, "Nay!"
The quite knyghte bede tho, "Do way,   *white; commanded then "Stop"*
450 For that quile have I bene here.   *while*
Thowe schild noghte mowrne no suche wise,
For God may bothe mon falle and rise,   *bring down and raise up*
For His helpe is evyrmore nere.
For gud His butte a lante lone,   *wealth is but a loaned gift*
455 Sumtyme men have hit, sumtyme none;
Thu hast full mony a pere.   *many an equal*

"Now thenke on Him, that deut on Rode.   *think; died on Cross*
That for us sched His precius blode,
For the and monkynd all.   *mankind*
460 For a mon that gevees him to god thewis,   *devotes himself to good habits*

Authir to gentilmen or to schrewis,   *Either; evil persons*
On summe side wille hit fall.   *In some respect*
A mon that hase all way bynne kynde,   *man*
Sum curtas mon yette may he fynde,   *courteous man*
465 That mekille may stonde in stalle;   *greatly; be of help*
Repente the noghte that thu hase done,   *what you have done*
For He that schope bothe sunne and mone,   *made*
Full wele may pay for alle."

Quod the quite knyghte, "Wold thu luffe him avre all thing   *love; over*
470 That wold the owte of thi mournyng bringe,   *out*
And kevyr the owte of kare?   *retrieve; out; sorrow*
For here beside duellus a riall king,   *nearby dwells; royal*
And hase a doghtur fayre and yinge,   *young*
He luffis nothing mare.   *loves; more*
475 And thu art one of the semelist knyghte   *fairest*
That evyr yette I see with syghte,
That any armes bare.
That mun no mon hur wedde ne weld,   *may; hold*
Butte he that first is inne the fild,   *field*
480 And best thenne justus thare.   *jousts*

"And thu schalt cum thedur als gay   *there as*
Als any erliche mon may,   *As; earthly*
Of thi sute schall be non;   *your class*
Thu schall have for thi giftus gevand,   *gifts given*
485 Grete lordus to thi honde,   *lords; at hand*
And loke thu spare righte none.
Thu say the menne that come with the,
That thay were drounet on the see,   *drowned; sea*
With wild waturs slone.   *waters slain*
490 Loke that thu be large of feyce,   *generous of rewards*
Tille thu have wonon gode congrece,   *group of attendants*
And I schall pay ichone."   *each one*

He sayd, "That thu be fre of wage,   *generous; payment*
And I schall pay for thi costage,   *expense*
495 Ten thowsand gif thu ladde.   *undertake*
Ther schall thu wynne full mekille honowre,   *great honor*
Fild and frithe, towne and towre,   *Field; woods; town; tower*
That lady schall thu wedde.
And sithun I schall come agayne to the,   *later*
500 Qwen thu hase come thi frindus to see,   *When; your friends*
In stid quere thu art stadde.   *In place where; set*
Butte a forwart make I with the or that thu goe,   *covenant; before*
That evyn to part betwene us toe   *evenly to divide; two*
The godus thu hase wonun and spedde."   *goods; won; obtained*

505	Thenne bespeke Sir Amadace,
	"And thu have myghte thrughe Goddus grace
	So to cumford to me,
	Thu schalt fynde me true and lele
	And evyn, lord, for to dele
510	Betwix the and me."
	"Fare wele," he sayd, "Sir Amadace!
	And thu schall wurche thrughe Goddus grace,
	And hit schall be with the."
	Sir Amadace sayd, "Have gode day,
515	And thu schall fynde me, and I may,
	Als true as any mon may be."

A Fitte

	Now als Sir Amadace welke bi the se sonde,	*walked by the sea sand*
	The broken schippus he ther fonde —	*ships*
	Hit were mervayl to say.	*marvel*
520	He fond wrekun amung the stones	*wrecked*
	Knyghtes in menevere for the nones,	*ceremonial trim; at that time*
	Stedes quite and gray,	*Horses white*
	With all kynne maner of richas	*richness*
	That any mon myghte devise	*imagine*
525	Castun uppe with waturs lay;	*Cast*
	Kistes and cofurs bothe ther stode,	*Chests; coffers*
	Was fulle of gold precius and gode,	
	No mon bare noghte away.	*bore*

	Thenne Sir Amadace he him cladde,	*dressed*
530	And that was in a gold webbe,	*woven cloth*
	A bettur myghte none be.	
	And the stede that he on rode,	
	Wasse the best that evyr mon hade	
	In justing for to see.	*jousting*
535	Ther he wanne full mecul honoure,	*won; great*
	Fild and frithe, toune and towre,	*Field; wood; town; tower*
	Castell and riche cité.	
	Aure that gud he hovet full ryghte.	*Above; lingered*
	That see the king and his doghtur bryghte,	*saw; lovely*
540	The justing furthe schild be.	*should*

	The kinge sayd to his doghtur bryghte,	
	"Lo, yond hoves a riall knyghte!"	*lingers; royal*
	A messyngere he ches,	*chose*
	His aune squier, and knyghtes thre,	*own*
545	And bede, "Go loke quat yone may be,	*commanded; what over there*
	And telle me quo hit is.	*who*
	And his gud hitte schall be tente	*welfare; attended to*

	Holly to his cummawundemente,	*Wholly; command*
	Certan withoutun lesse.	*lies*
550	Go we to his comyng all togethir,	
	And say that he is welcum hethir,	
	And he be comun o pese."	*If; come in peace*

	As the messingerus welke bi the see sonde,	*messengers walked; seashore*
	Thay toke Sir Amadace bi the quite honde,	*white*
555	And tithinges conne him fraynne:	*asked him about himself*
	And sayd, "Oure lord, the king, hase send us hethir	
	To wete youre comyng all togethir,	*know of*
	And ye wold us sayn.	*If; tell*
	He says your gud hitte schall be tente,	*attended to*
560	Holly atte youre commawundemente,	*Wholly; command*
	Certan is noghte to layne.	*conceal*
	Quatsever ye wille with the kinges men do,	*Whatever*
	Yo thar butte commawunde hom therto,	*command them*
	And have servandis full bayne."	*servants; accommodating*

565	And Sir Amadace sayd, "I wasse a prince of mekil pride,	*great*
	And here I hade thoghte to ryde,	
	Forsothe atte this journay.	
	I was vetaylet with wyne and flowre,	*supplied*
	Hors, stedus, and armoure,	
570	Knyghtus of gode aray.	
	Stithe stormes me oredrofe,	*Strong; overthrew*
	Mi nobull schippe hit all torofe,	*tore apart*
	Tho sothe youreselvun may say.	*truth; see*
	To spend I have enughe plenté,	
575	Butte all the men that come with me,	
	Forsothe thai bynne away."	*are away (lost)*

	Then Sir Amadace, that wasse so stithe on stede,	*strong*
	To the castell gates thay conne him lede,	*began*
	And told the king all the cace.	*case (situation)*
580	The king sayd, "Thu art welcum here,	
	I rede the be full gud chere,	*advise*
	Thonke Jhesu of His grace.	*Thank*
	Seche a storme as thu was inne,	
	That thu myghte any socur wynne,	*succor*
585	A full fayre happe hit wase.	*chance*
	I see nevyr man that sete in sete,	*sat in seat*
	So muche of my lufue myghte gete	*praise; get*
	As thu thiselvun hase."	*have*

	Thenne the king for Sir Amadace sake	
590	A riall cri thenne gerutte he make	*royal; caused*

Throoute in that cité.
To all that ther wold servyse have,
Knyghte, squiere, yoman and knave,   *yeoman*
Iche mon in thayre degré,   *Each man*
595   That wold duelle with Sir Amadace,   *abide*
Hade lost his men in a cace,   *accident*
And drownet hom on the se.   *drowned them*
He wold gif hom toe so muche, or ellus more,   *them; else*
As any lord wold evyr or quare,   *anywhere*
600   And thay wold with him be.   *If*

Quen gentilmen herd that cry,   *When*
Thay come to him full hastely,
With him for to be.
Be then the justing wasse alle cryed,   *By*
605   There was no lord ther besyde
Had halfe as mony men os he.   *as*
Ther he wanne so mycull honoure,   *won; great*
Fild and frithe, towne and toure,   *Field and forest*
Castell and riche cité;
610   A hundrithe sedis he wan and moe,   *hundred districts; won*
And gave the king the ton halve of thoe,   *one half of those*
Butte ther othir til his felo keput he.   *for his partner (i.e., the white knight); kept*

Quen the justing was all done,
To unarme hom thay wente anone,   *disarm*
615   Hastely and belyve,   *quickly*
Then sayd the king anon ryghte,
And bede, "Gromersy, gentull knyghte!"   *Many thanks*
Ofte and fele sithe.   *many times*
Then the kingus doghtur that wasse gente,   *fair*
620   Unlasutte the knyghte, to mete thay wente,   *Took the armor off; dinner*
All were thay gladde and blithe.   *happy*
Quen aythir of othir hade a sighte,   *When either*
Suche a lufue betuene hom lighte,   *love*
That partut nevyr thayre lyve.   *parted*

625   Quen thay hade etun, I understonde,   *eaten*
The king toke Sir Amadace bi the quite honde,   *white*
And to him conne he say:
"Sir," he sayd, "withoutun lesse,   *deceit*
I have a doghtur that myn ayre ho isse.   *my heir she is*
630   And ho be to yaure pay,   *If she; pleasure (reward)*
And ye be a mon that will wedde a wife,
I vouche hur safe, by my life,   *entrust*
On yo that fayre may.   *fair maiden*
Here a gifte schall I yo gife,

635   Halfe my kyndome quilles I life —   *while*
       Take all aftur my daye."

       "Gramarcy," seyd Sir Amadas,
       And thonkyd tho kyng of that grace,
       Of his gyfftes gudde.
640   Sone after, as y yow sey,
       To the kyrke yode thei   *church went*
       To wedde that frely fode.   *noble young warrior*
       Ther was gold gyffon in that stonde,   *given; at that time*
       And plenty of sylver, many a ponde,   *pound*
645   Be the way as thei yode.   *went*
       And after in hall thei satte all,
       Tho lordes and tho lades small   *young gentlemen*
       That comon wer of gentyll kyn.   *noble kin*

       Thus is Sir Amadace kevyrt of his wo,   *recovered*
650   That God lene grace, that we were so!   *grant*
       A riall fest gerut he make.   *royal; caused*
       Ther weddut he that lady brighte,   *wedded*
       The maungery last a faurtenyghte,   *feasting; fortnight*
       With schaftes for to schake.   *spears; shake*
655   Othir halfe yere thay lifd in gomun,   *joy*
       A fayre knave child hade thay somun,   *boy; together*
       Grete myrthes con thay make.   *began*
       Listuns now, lordinges, of anters grete,   *adventures*
       Quyll on a day before the mete   *While; dinner*
660   This felau come to the gate.   *fellow*

       He come in als gay gere,   *such; apparel*
       Ryghte as he an angell were,
       Cladde he was in quite.   *white*
       Unto the porter speke he thoe,   *then*
665   Sayd, "To thi lord myn ernde thu go,   *message*
       Hasteli and alstite.   *immediately*
       And if he frayne oghte aftur me,   *asks*
       For quethun I come, or quat cuntré,   *whence; what*
       Say him my sute is quite.   *suit; white*
670   And say we have togethir bene,
       I hope full wele he have me sene,   *expect; seen me*
       He wille hitte nevyr denyte."   *deny*

       Thenne the porter wente into the halle,
       Alsone his lord he metes withalle,   *As soon as*
675   He sailles him as he conne: *approaches; can*
       Sayd, "Lord, here is comun the fayrist knyghte,
       That evyr yette I see with syghte,

	Sethen I was market mon.	*man*
	Milke quite is his stede,	*white*
680	And so is all his other wede,	*clothing*
	That he hase opon.	
	He says ye have togethir bene,	
	I hope full well ye have him sene,	
	Butte with him is comun no mon."	

	"Is he comun," he sayd, "myn owun true fere?	*my own; companion*
685	To me is he bothe lefe and dere,	*beloved and dear*
	So aght him wele to be.	*ought*
	Butte, all my men, I yo commawunde,	*command*
	To serve him wele to fote and honde,	
690	Ryghte as ye wold do me."	
	Then Sir Amadace agaynus him wente,	*to*
	And allso did that ladi gente,	*fair*
	That was so bryghte of ble.	*lovely; face*
	And did wele that hur aghte to do;	*what she ought*
695	All that hur lord lufd wurschipput ho;	*loved she worshiped*
	All suche wemen wele myghte be.	*Such all women well might be*

	Quo schuld his stede to stabulle have?	*Who*
	Knyghte, squier, yoman ne knave,	
	Nauthir with him he broghte.	*None of these*
700	Thenne Sir Amadace wold have takyun his stede,	
	And to the halle himselvun lede,	
	Butte, so wold he noghte.	
	He sayd, "Sertan, the sothe to telle,	*Certain; truth*
	I will nauthir ete, drinke, no duelle,	*neither; remain*
705	Be God, that me dere boghte.	*By; dearly bought (redeemed)*
	Butte take and dele hit evun in toe,	*But; divide; two*
	Gif me my parte, and lette me goe,	
	Gif I be wurthi oghte."	*If I be worthy of anything*

	Thenne spoke Sir Amadace so fre,	
710	"For Goddus luffe, lette suche wurdus be!	*love; let; words*
	Thay grevun my herte full sore.	*grieve*
	For we myghte noghte this faurtenyghte	*fortnight*
	Owre rich londus dele and dighte,	*divide; prepare*
	Thay liun so wide quare.	*lie; broadly here and there*
715	Butte lette us leng together here,	*abide*
	Righte as we brethir were,	*Just as if we were brothers*
	As all thin one hit ware.	*thine (your) own*
	And othir gates noghte part will wee,	*otherwise*
	Butte atte thi will, sir, all schall bee;	
720	Goddes forbote, Sir, thou hit spare!"	*refrain from using it*

He sayd, "Broke wele thi londus brode,   *Enjoy*
Thi castels hee, thi townus made,   *high*
Of hom kepe I righte none;
Allso thi wuddus, thi waturs clere,   *your woods*
725   Thi frithis, thi forestus, fer and nere,   *woods; forests far and near*
Thi ringus with riche stone,   *rings*
Allso thi silvyr, thi gold rede,   *enjoy*
For hit may stonde me in no stidde,
I squere, bi Sayn John!   *swear*
730   But, be my faythe, wothoutun stryve,   *without strife*
Half thi child, and halfe thi wyve,   *Divide; divide*
And thay schall with me gone."

"Alas!" sayd Sir Amadace than,
"That evyr I this woman wan,   *won*
735   Or any wordes gode.
For His life, that deet on tre,   *died on tree (Cross)*
Quatsever ye will, do with me,   *Whatsoever*
For Him that deet on Rode.   *died on Cross*
Ye, take all that evyr I have
740   Wythe thi, that ye hur life save."   *If only; you her*
Thenne the knyghte wele undurstode,
And squere, "Be God, that me dere boghte,   *swore; dearly bought (redeemed)*
Othir of thi thinge then kepe I noghte,
Off all thi wordes gode!

745   Butte thenke on thi covenand that thu made   *covenant*
In the wode, quen thu mestur hade,   *when; need*
How fayre thu hettus me thare!"   *entreated*
Sir Amadace sayd, "I wotte, hit was soe,   *know*
But my lady for to sloe,   *slay*
750   Me thinke grete synne hit ware."
Then the lady undurstode anon,
The wurd that was betwene hom,   *promise; them*
And grevyt hur nevyr the more.   *grieved*
Then ladi sayd, "For His luffe thet deut on tre,   *love; died on tree (Cross)*
755   Loke youre covandus holdun be,   *See that covenant be held (kept)*
Goddes forbotte ye me spare!"   *forbid*

Thenne bespeke that ladi brighte,
Sayd, "Ye schall him hold that ye have highte,   *promised*
Be God, and Sayn Drightine!   *Holy Lord*
760   For His lufe that deet on tre,   *love; died on tree (Cross)*
Loke yaure covandus holdun be,   *covenant be held (kept)*
Yore forward was full fyne.   *agreement; proper*
Sithun Crist will that hit be so,
Take and parte me evun in toe,   *two*

765   Thu wan me and I am thine.
      Goddus fobotte that ye hade wyvut,   *forbid; wived*
      That I schuld yo a lure makette,   *temptation (bait)*
      Yore wurschip in londe to tyne!"   *lose*

      Still ho stode, withoutun lette,   *she*
770   Nawthir changet chere, ne grette,   *Neither changed expression, nor wept*
      That lady myld and dere.
      Bede, "Foche me my yung sun me beforne,   *Commanded, "Fetch*
      For he was of my bodi borne,
      And lay my herte full nere."
775   "Now," quod the quite knyghte thare,
      "Quethur of hom luffus thu mare?"   *Which; them; love; more*
      He sayd, "My wife, so dere!"
      "Sithun thu luffus hur the more,   *love*
      Thu schalt parte hur evyn before,   *divide her evenly*
780   Hur quite sidus in sere."   *white; apart*

      Thenne quen Sir Amadace see   *when*
      That no bettur hitte myghte bee,
      He ferd as ho were wode.   *behaved; mad*
      Thenne all the mene in that halle,
785   Doune on squonyng ther con thay falle,   *swooning*
      Before thayre lord thay stode.
      The burd was broghte that schuld hur on dele;   *board; divide*
      Ho kissute hur lord sithis fele,   *She kissed; times many*
      And sithun therto ho yode.   *afterwards; she went*
790   Ho layd hur downe mekely enughe,   *She*
      A cloth then aure hur enyn thay droghe;   *over her eyes*
      That lady was myld of mode.   *calm of spirit*

      Thenne the quite knyghte, "I will do the no unskill,   *white; wrong*
      Thu schalt dele hit atte thi wille,   *divide*
795   The godus that here now is."   *goods*
      Thenne speke Sir Amadace so fre,   *gracious*
      Sayd, "Atte your wille, lord, all schall be,
      And so I hope hit is."
      Then Sir Amadace a squrd uppehente,   *sword took up*
800   To strike the ladi was his entente,
      And thenne the quite knyghte bede "Sese!"   *white; bade; Stop*
      He toke uppe the ladi, and the litull knave,
      And to Sir Amadace ther he hom gave,   *them*
      And sayd, "Now is tyme of pees!"   *peace*

805   He sayd, "I con notte wite the gif thu were woe,   *blame you if; distressed*
      Suche a ladi for to slo,   *slay*
      Thi wurschip thus wold save.

Yette I was largely as gladde,
Quen thu gafe all that evyr thu hade,   *When*
810   My bones for to grave.   *bury*
In a chapell quere I lay to howundus mete,   *where; as hounds' food*
Thu payut furst thritty powund by grete,   *paid; in full*
Sethun all that thu myghtus have.   *Then*
Ther I besoghte God schuld kevyr the of thi care,   *remove*
815   That for me hade made the so bare,
Mi wurschip in lond to save."   *honor*

"Fare wele now," he sayd, "mynne awne true fere!   *own; friend*
For my lenging is no lengur her,   *dwelling; longer here*
With tunge sum I the telle.
820   Butte loke thu lufe this lady as thi lyve,   *love*
That thus mekely, withouten stryve,   *without strife*
Thi forwardus wold fulfille."   *promises*
Thenne he wente oute of that toune,
He glode away as dew in towne,   *went*
825   And thay abode ther stille.
Thay knelutte downe opon thayre kne,   *knelt*
And thonket God and Mary fre,   *thanked; gracious*
And so thay hade gud skille.

Thenne Sir Amadace and his wive,
830   With joy and blis thay ladde thayre live,
Unto thayre ending daye.
Ther is ladis now in lond full foe   *few*
That wold have servut hor lord soe,
Butte sum wold have sayd nay.
835   Botte quoso serves God truly,   *whoever*
And His modur, Mary fre,
This dar I savely say: *safely*
Gif hom sumtyme like full ille,   *If them*
Yette God will graunte hom all hor wille,   *them; their*
840   Tille hevyn the redy waye.   *To*

Then Sir Amadace send his messingerus,
All the londus ferre and nere,   *far and near*
Unto his awne cuntré.   *own*
Till all that evyr his lond withheld,
845   Frithe or forest, towne or filde,   *Woods; field*
With tresur owte boghte he.   *He repaid his debts with money*
His stuard and othir, that with him were,
He send aftur hom, as ye may here,   *them*
And gafe hom gold and fee.   *them; riches*
850   And thay ther with him for to leng,   *remain*

Evyrmore till thayre lyvus ende,
With myrthe and solempnité.   *joy; proper ceremony*

Thenne sone aftur the kinge deet, atte Goddus wille,   *died*
And thay abode thare stille,
855   As ye schall undurstond.
Thenne was he lord of toure and towne,
And all thay comun to his somoune,   *summons*
All the grete lordus of the londe.
Thenne Sir Amadace, as I yo say,
860   Was crownette kinge opon a day,   *crowned*
Wyth gold so clure schinand.   *brilliantly shining*
Jhesu Criste in Trinité,   *Trinity*
Blesse and glade this cumpany,   *make happy*
And ore us halde His hande!   *over*

Finis de Sir Amadace

❧ NOTES TO *SIR AMADACE*

I have used the following abbreviations in these textual and explanatory notes: **A**: Advocates Manuscript; **B**: Christopher Brookhouse, ed., *Sir Amadace and The Avowyng of Arthur*; **IR**: Ireland Manuscript; **M**: Maldwyn Mills, ed., *Six Middle English Romances*; **MED**: *Middle English Dictionary*; **P**: Ad Putter, "Gifts and Commodities:" **R**: John Robson, ed., *Three Early English Metrical Romances*; **W**: Henry Weber, ed., *Metrical Romances of the Thirteenth, Fourteenth, and Fifteenth Centuries*.

I have based my text on the Ireland Manuscript (c. 1450) following R, B, M. There are notable differences from the Advocates Manuscript (late fifteenth century), documented by R. W prints A. I have followed B, R in supplying some lines from A.

1	A leaf, containing four stanzas (24 lines) is missing from IR. It is clear, however, that Sir Amadace has put himself in financial jeopardy by excessive spending that is understood to be generosity rather than profligacy — a common didactic motif. A note has been inserted in IR explaining that a leaf is lost, but I have chosen to begin lineation with fol. 17, following the practice of past editors.
3	*be*. B: *þe*; R, M: *be*.
7	*Qu* for "wh" or "w" is common throughout. Third-person singular pasts in *-it* (e.g., *kennit*, line 18) and *-ut* (e.g., *ordanut*, line 50) are also common. For a detailed account of spelling and accidence see B, pp. 11–16.
11	*on*. B: *one*.
12	*Thaghe*. IR: *Thaȝghe*. M: *Thagh*.
29–30	Keeping one's debts a secret was a cardinal mercantile rule. See Chaucer's Shipman (VIII[B²]225–34). See notes to lines 34 and 48.
31	*wedsette*: to mortgage, to put one's land up as a pledge against debt (*OED*).
34	Compare Chaucer's Merchant "sownynge alwey th' encrees of his wynnyng" (I[A] 275) and his Shipman, who meticulously keeps his debts a secret, else he might have to flee the country. See note to line 48 below.
40	Sir Amadace's display of generosity creates more an image of affluence than charity as he prepares to go into hiding.
48	Compare Chaucer's Shipman who avows that he would have to pretend to go on "a pilgrimage, or goon out of the weye" (VII[B²] 230–34) if his *pryvetee* were known.

50, 56	R, B, M inserted the *a*.
60	P argues that the story of *Sir Amadace* is designed to "exemplify the wisdom and ultimate profitability of reckless spending" (371), thereby creating an enduring body of indebtedness and gratitude (similar to that of a blood-brother relationship) between Sir Amadace and the White Knight/merchant. This celebration of generosity is based on the religious belief that one does not own goods, and espouses a gift economy in which "repaying kindness does not cancel gratitude but only engages the giver's gratitude in return" (P, pp. 374, 394).
81	*hur*. IR originally reads *his*, which is deleted and changed to *hur*.
93	*no*. B: *so*.
96	*my*. B: *me*.
97	IR, M: *Amace*. B notes the mark in IR indicating that the scribe intended to correct the word. I have corrected to *Amadace*.
	squier. B: *squir*.
121	*his*. B: *is*.
129	IR, M: *A*; I have followed R. B: *And*.
134	*mon*. Omitted by B.
143	*rowunde*: a round minted coin. *MED* lists this alternative spelling which is consistent with the dialect and orthographical patterns of the poem.
157	The lady's explanation parallels Sir Amadace's situation. Here is the first reference to *fole* (fool), which will become Amadace's role.
172	*telle that he seke lay*. B silently "emends" to *tell that seke he lay*.
204	IR inserts *A Fitte* at the end of this line and at the end of line 516.
206	*he*. B: *me*.
212	*I will*. IR: *will*. Acephalous syntax (the dropping of a subject pronoun) commonly occurs in Middle English. R's emendation, followed by B, M, and me.
225	According to P, Sir Amadace does not see his gift to the White Knight/merchant as a loss, but as a "conversion of real capital into 'gret merit,' an entitlement to gratitude and future reward that binds one to other bearers of this 'symbolic capital.' By refusing to invest in 'merit,' the merchant excludes himself from the community of givers, a community whose founding member is of course God himself" (379).
237	R, B, M insert *The . . . the*.
246	*womon*. B: *woman*.
250	*thritti powunde*. Perhaps a loose analogue to Judas' selling of Jesus for thirty pieces of silver lurks in the background here as Amadace kindly uses the sum to redeem the lady and her knight, rather than betray them, even though it is all

that he has. Rather than being like Judas, he's like the widow with her mite, which goes for charity.

260   B (p. 103) explains the ancient tradition, preserved in folklore, of punishing a debtor by refusing burial. The practice had long since disappeared by the time of the poem. This section begins the "grateful dead" motif, wherein the hero finds and buries a previously unburied corpse. The ghost of the grateful dead person subsequently offers to help the hero on condition of receiving half of whatever reward is ultimately obtained. See G. H. Gerould, *The Grateful Dead*, Publications of the Folk-Lore Society 60 (London, 1908). Williams suggests that in this type of story, there are, in fact, two folk motifs operating: the "Grateful Dead" and the "Divided Winnings" ("*Sir Amadace*," p. 65). As a literary example of the "Grateful Dead" motif in isolation, Williams offers Cicero's story of Simonides who, having buried an exposed corpse, is warned in a dream not to set out to sea; those who ignore the warning are drowned. See also the *Book of Tobit*, the medieval French texts *Richard le Biaus* and the *Lion de Bourges*, and the fifteenth-century prose romance of *Oliver de Castille et Artus d'Algarbe*.

295   *Thritty prustus*. The singing of a "trental" was deemed the most efficacious of masses for the dead. Compare the boast of the friar in Chaucer's Summoner's Tale (III[D] 1724–28).

373–81   I have followed R, B in supplying lines 344–55 from A. Because M does not, his lineation is twelve lines lower from this point.

411   IR, R, B, M: *word*. I have emended to *world* on the grounds that the phrase is so common in this poem and elsewhere as to be formulaic.

414   *hit*. B: *his*.

429   IR reduplicates *in this*.

435   *no mon*. IR: *non*. R's emendation followed by M and me.

439   B, following IR, has this line between my lines 468 and 469. Shifting the line to this position not only creates two twelve-line stanzas but also clarifies the sequence in lines 436–41. The scribe may have skipped the line, then incorporated it later where it makes grammatical sense but leaves lines 436–41 somewhat obscure.

441   See note to line 260.

449   *tho*. Omitted by both R and B; M: *the[m]*.

453   This line is repeated in the IR following line 455.

455   R, B insert *have*. This line is written in the margin and in what appears to be a later hand.

486   *loke*. B: *like*.

500   *come*. Mills: *tome* (leisure) without explanation. It is frequently difficult to distinguish "c" from "t" in Middle English manuscripts. MED notes *come* as an erroneous variant of *tome* in MS Fairfax 3 of John Gower, *Confessio Amantis*, II, 2680.

504	*hase.* B omits the *e* here and in line 681.
510	*Betwix.* B: *Bettwix.*
561	*Certan.* R, B, M: *Sertan.*
569	*stedus* as opposed to "hors" are "warhorses" or "chargers" (*MED*).
571	*oredrofe.* "Overdriven," refering to violent motions of the sea (*MED*).
593	*yoman.* B: *yomon.* So too in line 698.
594	*degré.* B: *degree.*
629	IR, R, B: *My nayre*: As B notes, this is clearly a false juncture. Such disjunctures are common in Middle English manuscripts. I have corrected to *Myn ayre* as has M.
637–48	I have followed R, B to supply lines 575–86 from *Sir Amadas* (Advocates MS). Because M has not, his lineation is twenty-four lines from this point.
650	*lene.* B: *leue.*
685	IR, R, B: *my nowun*; I have read: *myn owun*, as has M. Clearly a false juncture.
699	*he.* B: *be.*
707	Within the "Grateful Dead" story type, there is no known literary source for the White Knight's threat to kill the wife and child of Sir Amadace. However, a similar plot climax does appear in the later *Olvier et Artus* (Williams, "*Sir Amadace*," p. 67).
709	*spoke.* R, M: *speke.*
717	*thin one.* IR, R, B: *thi none*; M: *thin one*. Correction of another false juncture.
719–20	B concludes line 719 with *thu hit spare*, taken from the end of line 720. He erroneously omits *all schall be / Goddes forbote, Sir*, and thus is a line short in this stanza.
759	*Sayn Drightine*: Holy Lord (from Old English).
786	*thay.* B: *that.*
801	*bede.* IR: *be*; I have followed R, B, M: *bede*. The test of obedience to his covenant parallels that of God's testing of Abraham (Genesis 22), where the father will slay his son rather than break his vow to God. Like Isaac, the child is spared when the angel bids "cease" and provides the redemptive substitution of a ram stuck in thorns, which medieval commentaries interpreted as a figuration of Him who died on the Cross. Perhaps this is why the poet sets Amadace's test on the Eve of Christ's nativity.
805	*woe.* B: *toe.*
812	*by.* B, M: *be.*
823	*toune.* B: *towne.*
845	IR, R, B: *of*. Although "of" is possible, "or" fits the familiar formula much better. M agrees.

❧ GLOSSARY

abigge *atone, redeem*
abuye *atone for*
ac *but, although*
aghte *owed*
agrame *angry*
aither *either, both*
aknes *on knees*
al bidene *all together*
Alemayne *Germany*
alien *anoint*
almest *almost*
also *as*
alstite *immediately, quickly*
amorwe *tomorrow, in the morning*
antur(s) *adventure(s)*
aplyght *truly; pledged*
ar *before*
araught *reached*
aschet *asked for*
asondri *asunder, apart*
aspie *notice, spy out*
astite *immediately, quickly*
astow *as you*
as wis as *surely, certainly*
atake *overtake*
ato, atuo *apart*
atten *finally*
atuinne *apart, separate*
authir *either, both*
avenaunt *attractive, agreeable,*
    beautiful, fortunate
avergon *die down*
avre *over*
awand *owing*
awe *dread*
awne *own*

bacine *basin*
bade *trouble*
bale *trouble*
bar(e) *bore*
bede *offer*
belyve *quickly*
bernes *young men, children, warriors*
bifel *occurred, happened*
bifelt *stayed*
bihight *promised*
bilapped *surrounded*
bileft *stayed*
bimene *lament*
bird *lady, woman*
birddes *ladies, women*
bistride *mount*
bitaught *commended*
bithenke *remember*
bitide *happen*
blawe *proclaim*
ble *countenance*
blesied *blessed*
blinne *cease*
blisced *blessed*
blisceing *blessing*
blithe *happy, graceful, joyful*
bode *warning*
bold *daring, courageous*
boon and blood *body*
borwe *castle; guarantor*
bote *relieve*
boteler(e) *dispenser (of food and drink)*
bounté *bounty, generosity*
bourd *jest*
boure, bowre *chamber, apartment*
bove *above*
braid *drew, unsheathed*

bright *lovely, attractive, glittering*
brini *coat of mail*
brushed *dressed, prepared*
busked *dressed, prepared*

cace *accident*
care *worry, trouble, care, grief*
careful *sorrowful*
casten *calculate(d)*
chaitif *coward*
chaumber, chaunber *private room*
chaungy *exchange*
chepeing *buying*
chere *appearance, mood, manner, disposition*
childer *children*
Cisyle *Sicily*
cleped *named, called*
cloth *clothing*
comly *noble, comely*
con *began*
consail, conseyl *secret(s)*
costage *expense*
countrai, cuntré *country*
coupes *cups*
couthe *could*
croudewain *pushcart*
crud *pushed*
curtais(e), curteis(e) *courteous, gracious, polite*

dathet *cursed*
dede *dead*
dede(e) *deed(s), action(s)*
defygured *disfigured, changed in appearance*
dempt *damned*
denyte *deny*
depe *deep; muddy*
derth *scarcity*
dight *set in order, prepare(d)*
diol *dole, sorrow*
diolful *doleful, sorrowful*
dole *alms*
doloure *sorrow, misfortune*
doughti, doughty *stouthearted, courageous*

dreri *sad, sorrowful*
droghe *drew*
dueling *delay*
duell *live, dwell*

echon, echoon *each one*
egre *fierce, bold*
eighen *eyes*
evell, *evil*
eventour *adventure*
everichdel *completely*

fain *joyful, gladly*
fale, fele *many*
fare *state*
fare *travel, live, go*
fare *fare(s)*
fay *faith*
febull *poor, feeble*
fede *eat*
feffet *endowed*
fel *occurred*
felawerede *fellowship*
felle *destroy*
felo *partner, colleague*
fer *fire*
fere *together*
ferli *terribly*
fert *afraid*
fest *feast*
fet *fetched*
feyce *rewards*
flote *drifted (in mind)*
fode *young man; fool*
fol *fool*
folesage *court fool*
fond *prove, ascertain, try*
foode *offspring*
forfare *destroy*
forlain *lain with*
forlore *utterly lost*
foryetun *forgotten*
foryif *forgive*
fouchoun, fauchon *long curved sword*
foules, fowles *birds*
fowle *disgraced*
franut *asked, inquired*

frayn(e) *ask, inquire*
fre(e) *generous, splendid, noble(man)*
frely *graciously, worthy*
frith(e) *woods*

gadelyng *rascal*
galwes *gallows*
gamen *play*
gan, gun *began to, caused to*
gat *conceived*
gente *fair*
gerutte *caused*
gest *story, stories; guest*
gete *goods*
getyn *conceived*
geyre *gear, equipment*
gile *guile*
gle *enjoy*
gome(s) *man (men)*
grame *harmful*
gret *great; greeted*
grille *fearsome*
grimli *horrible*

hend(e) *courteous, gracious, well-born, skillful; near (at hand)*
hendelich(e) *honorably*
hennes *hence*
hent *seized*
here *hair*
hight, hyght *promise, tell; named*
holtes *woods*
hom *them*
hote *named*
hove(d) *wait(ed)*
hoves (hovet) *lingers (ed)*
hyde *skin*

ibore *born*
ichon *each one*
ipult *brought down*
ischape *dressed*
iwis, iwys *certainly, I know*

jurnay, jorné, jurné *journey*
just(es) *joust(s)*

kan(ne) *knew*
keghte *incurred*
kend(e) *kin; kind; pleasing*
kest *put on, cast*
kin *kin, kind, kindly*
kithe *realize, slow, know*
knave *boy*
kyn, kynde *family, kin, kind*
kyneriche *kindred*

lare *teaching*
layne *conceal*
lazer *leper*
leeved *believed*
lef(e) *dear, agreeable*
leighth *lies*
lem *gleaming*
leman *lover, beloved*
lese *lose*
les(se) *lies, falsehood*
lesying *lying*
lettyyng *delay*
leueté *belief*
leve *beloved; permission*
levedi *lady*
libben *live*
liche, lyche *alike, similar*
liif *life*
lithe *listen, hear*
lodly *hideous*
loge, logging *dwelling*
lo(o)th(e) *unwilling, reluctant*
lordinges *lords*
lorn *lost, abandoned*
lourand *lowering*
lung *long*

main *force*
marchand *merchant*
mare *more, better*
may *maiden*
mecul *much, great*
mede *desire, reward*
meiné *household, retainers*
mekil *much, great*
mené *crowd, retainers*
menevere *ceremonial trim (dress)*

mengeth *troubles, disturbs*
menske *dignity*
menstracie *minstrelsy*
mesel *leper*
mest *most*
mete *food, meat*
mett *dreamed*
miche *much*
michel *great, size, greatness*
mild(e), myld(e) *mild, gentle*
miri(e) *pleasing, delightful*
mode, moode *manner, countenance,*
    frame of mind
mold *earth*
mon *moan, lament; man*
mow *may, will*
muchel *much, great*
mycull *much, great*

nace *nose*
naute *cattle*
nedelonges *necessarily*
neghteburs *neighbors*
nithe *envy, malice*
noither *neither, whether*
noricerie *nursery, child's room*

o, oon *one*
ogain *in return, again*
olive *alive*
on lyve *alive*
ond *indignation, anger*
ones *once*
onest *honest, fitting*
onus *once*
ordanut *prepared*
other *or*
otuain *apart*
overgon *die down*
oye *again*

palfrey *riding horse*
pight, pyght *adorned, decorated*
pines *pains*
plain *amuse*
plate *armor*
plight, plyght *plighted, pledge(d)*

pouer, pouwer, pover *poor*
pousté *power*
preke(d) *spur(red)*
pres *company, crowd*
prikeand *riding, galloping*
pris, priis, prys *excellent, prize*
pulput *royal pew*

queede *bad person*
quite *exonerated*
quyted *fulfilled, rewarded*

rade *rode*
red(e) *advice, counsel*
reede *read, counsel*
rekene *recount, reckon*
rere *collect*
resaive *receive, claim*
reweli *sad*
riall *royal*
rigge *back*
riis *branches*
Rode *Cross*
rowund(e) *round(s); coin(s)*

sailles *approaches*
sale *hall*
salit *saluted, greeted*
samned *gathered*
samyt *rich silk*
saveliche *except, only*
schaftes *spears*
schameliche *shameful(ly)*
scheld *shield*
schende *shame*
schond *shame; destroy*
schop *made*
schoren *shorn, shaved*
schour *pain*
schrede *equip, dress*
schuld *should, would*
semelist *fairest*
semly *in fine array, appropriately*
sere *part(s)*
serjaunt *man-at-arms*
sese(d) *give (gave), entrust(ed),*
    yield(ed)

sethen, sethun, sithun *since, afterwards; then; later*
sexteyn *sexton*
sey, seyghe *saw*
shuld *would, should*
sike *sick, ill*
sikeing *sighing*
sithe *time, instance*
sithun *afterwards, then, later*
skere *exonerated, cleared*
skille *excuse*
slo *fig, sloe, plum*
sloe, slon *slay*
solempneté *solemnity*
sometour *pack-horse driver*
sond *mercy*
sond(e) *message, messenger; mercy*
so(o)the *truth, truly*
sorn *sorrow*
spare *economize, spare*
spendutte *spent*
spille *kill, destroy*
spousy, spoused *espouse(d)*
sprad *covered*
squwyne *swine*
stede, stedus, stedes *horse(s); places*
stithe *strong*
stounde, stowunde *moment, time, instant, instance*
stroie *destroy*
stuard *steward*
susten *sustain, support*
swain *young man*
sweven *dream*
swithe *quickly*

teain, tuai *two, both*
tene *vexation; pain*
tente *attended to*
termente *interment*
thaghe *though*
the *the; you*
thennes *thence*
thewis *habits*
tho *then*
thoffe *though*
thole(d) *suffer(ed)*

tite *soon*
tithinges *news, tidings*
tobrent *burned*
todrawe *violate(d)*
tognaue *gnaw to pieces*
torende *tear*
torofe *tore apart*
toschiverd *broke into pieces*
traue *believe*
travayle *pain(s)*
trew(e) *faithful*
treye *trial*
Trinyté *Trinity*
trouth, treuthe, trewthe *truth, loyalty, fidelity*
trumpes *horns*
tuay, tuai, tway *two*

underfong *undertake*
unkouth *untaught, unaware*
unsemand *pretending*
unwrain *reveal*

vetaylet *supplied*
vouwed *vowed*

wald *would*
war(e) *aware, alert*
ware *were*
warld *world*
wede *clothing, dress; armor*
wele, weele *success, good fortune*
welke *walked*
wemme *blemish*
wend *believed*
wend(e) *go, travel*
wene *think*
wer *danger*
weyndut *went, wended*
whilom *at one time, once upon a time*
wight, wyght *brave, person*
withstode *withstood, persisted*
witte *find out*
wo(o) *sadness, ill fortune*
wode, wood *mad, crazy*
won *dwelling, possessions*
wond *hesitate*

wonyd *lived, resided*
worn *were*
worthli, worthy *deserving, stately, valuable*
wrake *trouble*
wray *betray*
wreke *avenge*
wrengand *wringing*
wrethe *wrath*
wrothlich *angrily*
wyght *person*
wynd *fared*

yaf *gave*
yare *fair; ready, prepared, readily*
yblisced *blessed*
ycleped *named, called*
ycorn *born, descended*
yede *went*
yere *before*
yhote *called*
yif, yive *if*
yode *went*
yplight *truly*
ywys *cetainly, indeed*

MIDDLE ENGLISH TEXTS SERIES

The Floure and the Leafe, The Assembly of Ladies, The Isle of Ladies, edited by Derek Pearsall (1990)

Three Middle English Charlemagne Romances, edited by Alan Lupack (1990)

Six Ecclesiastical Satires, edited by James M. Dean (1991)

Heroic Women from the Old Testament in Middle English Verse, edited by Russell A. Peck (1991)

The Canterbury Tales: Fifteenth-Century Continuations and Additions, edited by John M. Bowers (1992)

Gavin Douglas, *The Palis of Honoure*, edited by David Parkinson (1992)

Wynnere and Wastoure and The Parlement of the Thre Ages, edited by Warren Ginsberg (1992)

The Shewings of Julian of Norwich, edited by Georgia Ronan Crampton (1994)

King Arthur's Death: The Middle English Stanzaic Morte Arthur and Alliterative Morte Arthure, edited by Larry D. Benson, revised by Edward E. Foster (1994)

Lancelot of the Laik and Sir Tristrem, edited by Alan Lupack (1994)

Sir Gawain: Eleven Romances and Tales, edited by Thomas Hahn (1995)

The Middle English Breton Lays, edited by Anne Laskaya and Eve Salisbury (1995)

Sir Perceval of Galles and Ywain and Gawain, edited by Mary Flowers Braswell (1995)

Four Middle English Romances: Sir Isumbras, Octavian, Sir Eglamour of Artois, Sir Tryamour, edited by Harriet Hudson (1996; second edition 2006)

The Poems of Laurence Minot 1333–1352, edited by Richard H. Osberg (1996)

Medieval English Political Writings, edited by James M. Dean (1996)

The Book of Margery Kempe, edited by Lynn Staley (1996)

Amis and Amiloun, Robert of Cisyle, and Sir Amadace, edited by Edward E. Foster (1997; second edition 2007)

The Cloud of Unknowing, edited by Patrick J. Gallacher (1997)

Robin Hood and Other Outlaw Tales, edited by Stephen Knight and Thomas Ohlgren (1997; second edition 2000)

The Poems of Robert Henryson, edited by Robert L. Kindrick with assistance of Kristie A. Bixby (1997)

Moral Love Songs and Laments, edited by Susanna Greer Fein (1998)

John Lydgate, *Troy Book Selections*, edited by Robert R. Edwards (1998)

Thomas Usk, *The Testament of Love*, edited by R. Allen Shoaf (1998)

Prose Merlin, edited by John Conlee (1998)

Middle English Marian Lyrics, edited by Karen Saupe (1998)

John Metham, *Amoryus and Cleopes*, edited by Stephen F. Page (1999)

Four Romances of England: King Horn, Havelok the Dane, Bevis of Hampton, Athelston, edited by Ronald B. Herzman, Graham Drake, and Eve Salisbury (1999)

The Assembly of Gods: Le Assemble de Dyeus, or Banquet of Gods and Goddesses, with the Discourse of Reason and Sensuality, edited by Jane Chance (1999)

Thomas Hoccleve, *The Regiment of Princes*, edited by Charles R. Blyth (1999)

John Capgrave, *The Life of Saint Katherine*, edited by Karen A. Winstead (1999)

John Gower, *Confessio Amantis*, Vol. 1, edited by Russell A. Peck; with Latin translations by Andrew Galloway (2000; second edition 2006); Vol. 2 (2003); Vol. 3 (2004)

Richard the Redeless and Mum and the Sothsegger, edited by James M. Dean (2000)

Ancrene Wisse, edited by Robert Hasenfratz (2000)

Walter Hilton, *The Scale of Perfection*, edited by Thomas H. Bestul (2000)

John Lydgate, *The Siege of Thebes*, edited by Robert R. Edwards (2001)

Pearl, edited by Sarah Stanbury (2001)

The Trials and Joys of Marriage, edited by Eve Salisbury (2002)

Middle English Legends of Women Saints, edited by Sherry L. Reames, with assistance of Martha G. Blalock and Wendy R. Larson (2003)

The Wallace: Selections, edited by Anne McKim (2003)

Richard Maidstone, *Concordia (The Reconciliation of Richard II with London)*, edited by David R. Carlson, with a verse translation by A. G. Rigg (2003)

Three Purgatory Poems: The Gast of Gy, Sir Owain, The Vision of Tundale, edited by Edward E. Foster (2004)

William Dunbar, *The Complete Works*, edited by John Conlee (2004)

Chaucerian Dream Visions and Complaints, edited by Dana M. Symons (2004)

Stanzaic Guy of Warwick, edited by Alison Wiggins (2004)

Saints' Lives in Middle English Collections, edited by E. Gordon Whatley, with Anne B. Thompson and Robert K. Upchurch (2004)

Siege of Jerusalem, edited by Michael Livingston (2004)

The Kingis Quair and Other Prison Poems, edited by Linne R. Mooney and Mary-Jo Arn (2005)

Chaucerian Apocrypha: Selections, edited by Kathleen Forni (2005)

John Gower, *The Minor Latin Works*, edited and translated by R. F. Yeager, with *In Praise of Peace*, edited by Michael Livingston (2005)

Sentimental and Humorous Romances: Floris and Blancheflour, Sir Degrevant, The Squire of Low Degree, The Tournament of Tottenham, and The Feast of Tottenham, edited by Erik Kooper (2006)

Dicts and Sayings of the Philosophers, edited by John William Sutton (2006)

Everyman and Its Dutch Original, Elckerlijc, edited by Clifford Davidson, Martin W. Walsh, and Ton J. Broos (2006)

The N-Town Plays, edited by Douglas Sugano, with assistance by Victor I. Scherb (2007)

The Book of John Mandeville, edited by Tamarah Kohanski and C. David Benson (2007)

John Lydgate, *The Temple of Glas*, edited by J. Allan Mitchell (2007)

DOCUMENTS OF PRACTICE SERIES

Love and Marriage in Late Medieval London, selected, translated, and introduced by Shannon McSheffrey (1995)

Sources for the History of Medicine in Late Medieval England, selected, introduced, and translated by Carole Rawcliffe (1995)

A Slice of Life: Selected Documents of Medieval English Peasant Experience, edited, translated, and with an introduction by Edwin Brezette DeWindt (1996)

Regular Life: Monastic, Canonical, and Mendicant Rules, selected and introduced by Douglas J. McMillan and Kathryn Smith Fladenmuller (1997); second edition, selected and introduced by Daniel Marcel La Corte and Douglas J. McMillan (2004)

Women and Monasticism in Medieval Europe: Sisters and Patrons of the Cistercian Reform, selected, translated, and with an introduction by Constance H. Berman (2002)

Medieval Notaries and Their Acts: The 1327–1328 Register of Jean Holanie, introduced, edited, and translated by Kathryn L. Reyerson and Debra A. Salata (2004)

COMMENTARY SERIES

Haimo of Auxerre, *Commentary on the Book of Jonah*, translated with an introduction and notes by Deborah Everhart (1993)

Medieval Exegesis in Translation: Commentaries on the Book of Ruth, translated with an introduction and notes by Lesley Smith (1996)

Nicholas of Lyra's Apocalypse Commentary, translated with an introduction and notes by Philip D. W. Krey (1997)

Rabbi Ezra Ben Solomon of Gerona, *Commentary on the Song of Songs and Other Kabbalistic Commentaries*, selected, translated, and annotated by Seth Brody (1999)

John Wyclif, *On the Truth of Holy Scripture*, translated with an introduction and notes by Ian Christopher Levy (2001)

Second Thessalonians: Two Early Medieval Apocalyptic Commentaries, introduced and translated by Steven R. Cartwright and Kevin L. Hughes (2001)

The Glossa Ordinaria on the Song of Songs, translated with an introduction and notes by Mary Dove (2004)

MEDIEVAL GERMAN TEXTS IN BILINGUAL EDITIONS SERIES

Sovereignty and Salvation in the Vernacular, 1050–1150, introduction, translations, and notes by James A. Schultz (2000)

Ava's New Testament Narratives: "When the Old Law Passed Away," introduction, translation, and notes by James A. Rushing, Jr. (2003)

History as Literature: German World Chronicles of the Thirteenth Century in Verse, introduction, translation, and notes by R. Graeme Dunphy (2003)

VARIA

The Study of Chivalry: Resources and Approaches, edited by Howell Chickering and Thomas H. Seiler (1988)

Studies in the Harley Manuscript: The Scribes, Contents, and Social Contexts of British Library MS Harley 2253, edited by Susanna Fein (2000)

The Liturgy of the Medieval Church, edited by Thomas J. Heffernan and E. Ann Matter (2001); second edition (2005)

TO ORDER PLEASE CONTACT:

Medieval Institute Publications
Western Michigan University
Kalamazoo, MI 49008-5432
Phone (269) 387-8755
FAX (269) 387-8750

http://www.wmich.edu/medieval/mip/index.html

Medieval Institute Publications is a program
of The Medieval Institute, College of Arts
and Sciences, Western Michigan University

Typeset in 10/13 New Baskerville
with Golden Cockerel Ornaments display
Designed by Linda K. Judy
Manufactured by Sheridan Books, Inc.

Medieval Institute Publications
College of Arts and Sciences
Western Michigan University
1903 W. Michigan Avenue
Kalamazoo, MI 49008-5432
http://www.wmich.edu/medieval/mip

 WESTERN MICHIGAN UNIVERSITY